TABLE OF CONTENTS

Secret Key #1 - Time is Your Greatest Enemy ....

    Pace Yourself 6

Secret Key #2 - Guessing is not Guesswork 7

    Monkeys Take the Test 7

    $5 Challenge 8

Secret Key #3 - Practice Smarter, Not Harder 10

    Success Strategy 10

Secret Key #4 - Prepare, Don't Procrastinate 12

Secret Key #5 - Test Yourself 13

General Strategies 14

Top 20 Test Taking Tips 22

Introduction to the TExES Series 23

    Why am I required to take this TExES Assessment? 23

    Two Kinds of TExES Assessments 23

Reading and Understanding Text 24

    Identifying and Interpreting Figurative Language and Other Literary Elements ..24

    Identifying Patterns, Structures, and Characteristics of Literary Forms and Genres

   28

    Situating and Interpreting texts within their Historical and Cultural Context 30

    Identifying major works and authors of American, British, and World Literature

    from various cultures, genres, and periods 32

Helpful Tips for Reading and Understanding Text 34

    Skimming 34

    Paragraph Focus 35

    Eliminate Choices 36

    Contextual Clues 38

    Fact/Opinion 39

    Opposites 40

    New Information 41

Key Words 41

Language and Linguistics 42

Understanding the principles of language acquisition and development, including

social, cultural, and historical influences and the role of nature and dialects 42

Understanding Elements of the History and Development of the English Language

and American English 42

Understanding and Applying the elements of traditional grammar 43

Understanding the elements of semantics and how these elements affect meaning

.... 46

Composition and Rhetoric 47

Understanding and applying elements of teaching and writing 47

Understanding and Evaluating Rhetorical Features in Writing 49

Social Studies 51

Geography 51

World History 53

United States History 62

Government and Civics 67

Behavioral Sciences (Anthropology, Sociology, and Psychology) 69

Economics 71

Practice Test 77

Practice Questions 77

Answer Key and Explanations 103

Special Report: What Your Test Score Will Tell You About Your IQ 121

Special Report: Retaking the Test: What Are Your Chances at Improving Your Score?

.... 125

Special Report: What is Test Anxiety and How to Overcome It? 128

Lack of Preparation 128

Physical Signals 129

Nervousness 131

Study Steps 133

Helpful Techniques 137

Special Report: Additional Bonus Material 144

Secret Key #1 - Time is Your Greatest Enemy

Pace Yourself

Wear a watch. At the beginning of the test, check the time (or start a chronometer on your watch to count the minutes), and check the time after every few questions to make sure you are "on schedule."

If you are forced to speed up, do it efficiently. Usually one or more answer choices can be eliminated without too much difficulty. Above all, don't panic. Don't speed up and just begin guessing at random choices. By pacing yourself, and continually monitoring your progress against your watch, you will always know exactly how far ahead or behind you are with your available time. If you find that you are one minute behind on the test, don't skip one question without spending any time on it, just to catch back up. Take 15 fewer seconds on the next four questions, and after four questions you'll have caught back up. Once you catch back up, you can continue working each problem at your normal pace.

Furthermore, don't dwell on the problems that you were rushed on. If a problem was taking up too much time and you made a hurried guess, it must be difficult. The difficult questions are the ones you are most likely to miss anyway, so it isn't a big loss. It is better to end with more time than you need than to run out of time.

Lastly, sometimes it is beneficial to slow down if you are constantly getting ahead of time. You are always more likely to catch a careless mistake by working more slowly than quickly, and among very high-scoring test takers (those who are likely to have lots of time left over), careless errors affect the score more than mastery of material.

Secret Key #2 - Guessing is not Guesswork

You probably know that guessing is a good idea - unlike other standardized tests, there is no penalty for getting a wrong answer. Even if you have no idea about a question, you still have a 20-25% chance of getting it right.

Most test takers do not understand the impact that proper guessing can have on their score. Unless you score extremely high, guessing will significantly contribute to your final score.

Monkeys Take the Test

What most test takers don't realize is that to insure that 20-25% chance, you have to guess randomly. If you put 20 monkeys in a room to take this test, assuming they answered once per question and behaved themselves, on average they would get 20-25% of the questions correct. Put 20 test takers in the room, and the average will be much lower among guessed questions. Why?

1. The test writers intentionally writes deceptive answer choices that "look" right. A test taker has no idea about a question, so picks the "best looking" answer, which is often wrong. The monkey has no idea what looks good and what doesn't, so will consistently be lucky about 20-25% of the time.
2. Test takers will eliminate answer choices from the guessing pool based on a hunch or intuition. Simple but correct answers often get excluded, leaving a 0% chance of being correct. The monkey has no clue, and often gets lucky with the best choice.

This is why the process of elimination endorsed by most test courses is flawed and detrimental to your performance- test takers don't guess, they make an ignorant stab in the dark that is usually worse than random.

$5 Challenge

Let me introduce one of the most valuable ideas of this course- the $5 challenge:

You only mark your "best guess" if you are willing to bet $5 on it.
You only eliminate choices from guessing if you are willing to bet $5 on it.

Why $5? Five dollars is an amount of money that is small yet not insignificant, and can really add up fast (20 questions could cost you $100). Likewise, each answer choice on one question of the test will have a small impact on your overall score, but it can really add up to a lot of points in the end.

The process of elimination IS valuable. The following shows your chance of guessing it right:

If you eliminate wrong answer choices until only this many remain:	1	2	3
Chance of getting it correct:	100%	50%	33%

However, if you accidentally eliminate the right answer or go on a hunch for an incorrect answer, your chances drop dramatically: to 0%. By guessing among all the answer choices, you are GUARANTEED to have a shot at the right answer.

That's why the $5 test is so valuable- if you give up the advantage and safety of a pure guess, it had better be worth the risk.

What we still haven't covered is how to be sure that whatever guess you make is truly random. Here's the easiest way:

Always pick the first answer choice among those remaining.

Such a technique means that you have decided, **before you see a single test question**, exactly how you are going to guess- and since the order of choices tells you nothing about which one is correct, this guessing technique is perfectly random.

This section is not meant to scare you away from making educated guesses or eliminating choices- you just need to define when a choice is worth eliminating. The $5 test, along with a pre-defined random guessing strategy, is the best way to make sure you reap all of the benefits of guessing.

Secret Key #3 - Practice Smarter, Not Harder

Many test takers delay the test preparation process because they dread the awful amounts of practice time they think necessary to succeed on the test. We have refined an effective method that will take you only a fraction of the time.

There are a number of "obstacles" in your way to succeed. Among these are answering questions, finishing in time, and mastering test-taking strategies. All must be executed on the day of the test at peak performance, or your score will suffer. The test is a mental marathon that has a large impact on your future.

Just like a marathon runner, it is important to work your way up to the full challenge. So first you just worry about questions, and then time, and finally strategy:

Success Strategy

1. Find a good source for practice tests.
2. If you are willing to make a larger time investment, consider using more than one study guide- often the different approaches of multiple authors will help you "get" difficult concepts.
3. Take a practice test with no time constraints, with all study helps "open book." Take your time with questions and focus on applying strategies.
4. Take a practice test with time constraints, with all guides "open book."
5. Take a final practice test with no open material and time limits

If you have time to take more practice tests, just repeat step 5. By gradually exposing yourself to the full rigors of the test environment, you will condition your mind to the stress of test day and maximize your success.

Secret Key #4 - Prepare, Don't Procrastinate

Let me state an obvious fact: if you take the test three times, you will get three different scores. This is due to the way you feel on test day, the level of preparedness you have, and, despite the test writers' claims to the contrary, some tests WILL be easier for you than others.

Since your future depends so much on your score, you should maximize your chances of success. In order to maximize the likelihood of success, you've got to prepare in advance. This means taking practice tests and spending time learning the information and test taking strategies you will need to succeed.

Never take the test as a "practice" test, expecting that you can just take it again if you need to. Feel free to take sample tests on your own, but when you go to take the official test, be prepared, be focused, and do your best the first time!

Secret Key #5 - Test Yourself

Everyone knows that time is money. There is no need to spend too much of your time or too little of your time preparing for the test. You should only spend as much of your precious time preparing as is necessary for you to get the score you need.

Once you have taken a practice test under real conditions of time constraints, then you will know if you are ready for the test or not.

If you have scored extremely high the first time that you take the practice test, then there is not much point in spending countless hours studying. You are already there.

Benchmark your abilities by retaking practice tests and seeing how much you have improved. Once you score high enough to guarantee success, then you are ready.

If you have scored well below where you need, then knuckle down and begin studying in earnest. Check your improvement regularly through the use of practice tests under real conditions. Above all, don't worry, panic, or give up. The key is perseverance!

Then, when you go to take the test, remain confident and remember how well you did on the practice tests. If you can score high enough on a practice test, then you can do the same on the real thing.

General Strategies

The most important thing you can do is to ignore your fears and jump into the test immediately- do not be overwhelmed by any strange-sounding terms. You have to jump into the test like jumping into a pool- all at once is the easiest way.

Make Predictions

As you read and understand the question, try to guess what the answer will be. Remember that several of the answer choices are wrong, and once you begin reading them, your mind will immediately become cluttered with answer choices designed to throw you off. Your mind is typically the most focused immediately after you have read the question and digested its contents. If you can, try to predict what the correct answer will be. You may be surprised at what you can predict.

Quickly scan the choices and see if your prediction is in the listed answer choices. If it is, then you can be quite confident that you have the right answer. It still won't hurt to check the other answer choices, but most of the time, you've got it!

Answer the Question

It may seem obvious to only pick answer choices that answer the question, but the test writers can create some excellent answer choices that are wrong. Don't pick an answer just because it sounds right, or you believe it to be true. It MUST answer the question. Once you've made your selection, always go back and check it against the question and make sure that you didn't misread the question, and the answer choice does answer the question posed.

Benchmark

After you read the first answer choice, decide if you think it sounds correct or not. If it doesn't, move on to the next answer choice. If it does, mentally mark that answer choice. This doesn't mean that you've definitely selected it as your answer choice, it just means that it's the best you've seen thus far. Go ahead and read the next choice. If the next choice is worse than the one you've already selected, keep going to the next answer choice. If the next choice is better than the choice you've already selected, mentally mark the new answer choice as your best guess.

The first answer choice that you select becomes your standard. Every other answer choice must be benchmarked against that standard. That choice is correct until proven otherwise by another answer choice beating it out. Once you've decided that no other answer choice seems as good, do one final check to ensure that your answer choice answers the question posed.

Valid Information

Don't discount any of the information provided in the question. Every piece of information may be necessary to determine the correct answer. None of the information in the question is there to throw you off (while the answer choices will certainly have information to throw you off). If two seemingly unrelated topics are discussed, don't ignore either. You can be confident there is a relationship, or it wouldn't be included in the question, and you are probably going to have to determine what is that relationship to find the answer.

Avoid "Fact Traps"

Don't get distracted by a choice that is factually true. Your search is for the answer that answers the question. Stay focused and don't fall for an answer that is true but incorrect. Always go back to the question and make sure you're choosing an answer that actually answers the question and is not just a true statement. An answer can be factually correct, but it MUST answer the question asked. Additionally, two answers can both be seemingly correct, so be sure to read all of the answer choices, and make sure that you get the one that BEST answers the question.

Milk the Question

Some of the questions may throw you completely off. They might deal with a subject you have not been exposed to, or one that you haven't reviewed in years. While your lack of knowledge about the subject will be a hindrance, the question itself can give you many clues that will help you find the correct answer. Read the question carefully and look for clues. Watch particularly for adjectives and nouns describing difficult terms or words that you don't recognize. Regardless of if you completely understand a word or not, replacing it with a synonym either provided or one you more familiar with may help you to understand what the questions are asking. Rather than wracking your mind about specific detailed information concerning a difficult term or word, try to use mental substitutes that are easier to understand.

The Trap of Familiarity

Don't just choose a word because you recognize it. On difficult questions, you may not recognize a number of words in the answer choices. The test writers don't put "make-believe" words on the test; so don't think that just because you only recognize all the words in one answer choice means that answer choice must be correct. If you only recognize words in one answer choice, then focus on that one. Is it correct? Try your best to determine if it is correct. If it is, that is great, but if it doesn't, eliminate it. Each word and answer choice you eliminate increases your chances of getting the question correct, even if you then have to guess among the unfamiliar choices.

Eliminate Answers

Eliminate choices as soon as you realize they are wrong. But be careful! Make sure you consider all of the possible answer choices. Just because one appears right, doesn't mean that the next one won't be even better! The test writers will usually put more than one good answer choice for every question, so read all of them. Don't worry if you are stuck between two that seem right. By getting down to just two remaining possible choices, your odds are now 50/50. Rather than wasting too much time, play the odds. You are guessing, but guessing wisely, because you've been able to knock out some of the answer choices that you know are wrong. If you are eliminating choices and realize that the last answer choice you are left with is also obviously wrong, don't panic. Start over and consider each choice again. There may easily be something that you missed the first time and will realize on the second pass.

Tough Questions

If you are stumped on a problem or it appears too hard or too difficult, don't waste time. Move on! Remember though, if you can quickly check for obviously incorrect answer choices, your chances of guessing correctly are greatly improved. Before you completely give up, at least try to knock out a couple of possible answers. Eliminate what you can and then guess at the remaining answer choices before moving on.

Brainstorm

If you get stuck on a difficult question, spend a few seconds quickly brainstorming. Run through the complete list of possible answer choices. Look at each choice and ask yourself, "Could this answer the question satisfactorily?" Go through each answer choice and consider it independently of the other. By systematically going through all possibilities, you may find something that you would otherwise overlook. Remember that when you get stuck, it's important to try to keep moving.

Read Carefully

Understand the problem. Read the question and answer choices carefully. Don't miss the question because you misread the terms. You have plenty of time to read each question thoroughly and make sure you understand what is being asked. Yet a happy medium must be attained, so don't waste too much time. You must read carefully, but efficiently.

Face Value

When in doubt, use common sense. Always accept the situation in the problem at face value. Don't read too much into it. These problems will not require you to make huge leaps of logic. The test writers aren't trying to throw you off with a cheap trick. If you have to go beyond creativity and make a leap of logic in order to have an answer choice answer the question, then you should look at the other answer choices. Don't overcomplicate the problem by creating theoretical relationships or explanations that will warp time or space. These are normal problems rooted in reality. It's just that the applicable relationship or explanation may not be readily apparent and you have to figure things out. Use your common sense to interpret anything that isn't clear.

Prefixes

If you're having trouble with a word in the question or answer choices, try dissecting it. Take advantage of every clue that the word might include. Prefixes and suffixes can be a huge help. Usually they allow you to determine a basic meaning. Pre- means before, post- means after, pro - is positive, de- is negative. From these prefixes and suffixes, you can get an idea of the general meaning of the word and try to put it into context. Beware though of any traps. Just because con is the opposite of pro, doesn't necessarily mean congress is the opposite of progress!

Hedge Phrases

Watch out for critical "hedge" phrases, such as likely, may, can, will often, sometimes, often, almost, mostly, usually, generally, rarely, sometimes. Question writers insert these hedge phrases to cover every possibility. Often an answer choice will be wrong simply because it leaves no room for exception. Avoid answer choices that have definitive words like "exactly," and "always".

Switchback Words

Stay alert for "switchbacks". These are the words and phrases frequently used to alert you to shifts in thought. The most common switchback word is "but". Others include although, however, nevertheless, on the other hand, even though, while, in spite of, despite, regardless of.

New Information

Correct answer choices will rarely have completely new information included. Answer choices typically are straightforward reflections of the material asked about and will directly relate to the question. If a new piece of information is included in an answer choice that doesn't even seem to relate to the topic being asked about, then that answer choice is likely incorrect. All of the information needed to answer the question is usually provided for you, and so you should not have to make guesses that are unsupported or choose answer choices that require unknown information that cannot be reasoned on its own.

Time Management

On technical questions, don't get lost on the technical terms. Don't spend too much time on any one question. If you don't know what a term means, then since you don't have a dictionary, odds are you aren't going to get much further. You should immediately recognize terms as whether or not you know them. If you don't, work with the other clues that you have, the other answer choices and terms provided, but don't waste too much time trying to figure out a difficult term.

Contextual Clues

Look for contextual clues. An answer can be right but not correct. The contextual clues will help you find the answer that is most right and is correct. Understand the context in which a phrase or statement is made. This will help you make important distinctions.

Don't Panic

Panicking will not answer any questions for you. Therefore, it isn't helpful. When you first see the question, if your mind goes blank, take a deep breath. Force yourself to mechanically go through the steps of solving the problem and using the strategies you've learned.

Pace Yourself

Don't get clock fever. It's easy to be overwhelmed when you're looking at a page full of questions, your mind is full of random thoughts and feeling confused, and the clock is ticking down faster than you would like. Calm down and maintain the pace that you have set for yourself. As long as you are on track by monitoring your pace, you are guaranteed to have enough time for yourself. When you get to the last few minutes of the test, it may seem like you won't have enough time left, but if you only have as many questions as you should have left at that point, then you're right on track!

Answer Selection

The best way to pick an answer choice is to eliminate all of those that are wrong, until only one is left and confirm that is the correct answer. Sometimes though, an answer choice may immediately look right. Be careful! Take a second to make sure that the other choices are not equally obvious. Don't make a hasty mistake. There are only two times that you should stop before checking other answers. First is when you are positive that the answer choice you have selected is correct. Second is when time is almost out and you have to make a quick guess!

Check Your Work

Since you will probably not know every term listed and the answer to every question, it is important that you get credit for the ones that you do know. Don't miss any questions through careless mistakes. If at all possible, try to take a second to look back over your answer selection and make sure you've selected the correct answer choice and haven't made a costly careless mistake (such as marking an answer choice that you didn't mean to mark). This quick double check should more than pay for itself in caught mistakes for the time it costs.

Beware of Directly Quoted Answers

Sometimes an answer choice will repeat word for word a portion of the question or reference section. However, beware of such exact duplication – it may be a trap!

More than likely, the correct choice will paraphrase or summarize a point, rather than being exactly the same wording.

Slang

Scientific sounding answers are better than slang ones. An answer choice that begins "To compare the outcomes…" is much more likely to be correct than one that begins "Because some people insisted…"

Extreme Statements

Avoid wild answers that throw out highly controversial ideas that are proclaimed as established fact. An answer choice that states the "process should used in certain situations, if…" is much more likely to be correct than one that states the "process should be discontinued completely." The first is a calm rational statement and doesn't even make a definitive, uncompromising stance, using a hedge word "if" to provide wiggle room, whereas the second choice is a radical idea and far more extreme.

Answer Choice Families

When you have two or more answer choices that are direct opposites or parallels, one of them is usually the correct answer. For instance, if one answer choice states "x increases" and another answer choice states "x decreases" or "y increases," then those two or three answer choices are very similar in construction and fall into the same family of answer choices. A family of answer choices is when two or three answer choices are very similar in construction, and yet often have a directly opposite meaning. Usually the correct answer choice will be in that family of answer choices. The "odd man out" or answer choice that doesn't seem to fit the parallel construction of the other answer choices is more likely to be incorrect.

Top 20 Test Taking Tips

1. Carefully follow all the test registration procedures
2. Know the test directions, duration, topics, question types, how many questions
3. Setup a flexible study schedule at least 3-4 weeks before test day
4. Study during the time of day you are most alert, relaxed, and stress free
5. Maximize your learning style; visual learner use visual study aids, auditory learner use auditory study aids
6. Focus on your weakest knowledge base
7. Find a study partner to review with and help clarify questions
8. Practice, practice, practice
9. Get a good night's sleep; don't try to cram the night before the test
10. Eat a well balanced meal
11. Know the exact physical location of the testing site; drive the route to the site prior to test day
12. Bring a set of ear plugs; the testing center could be noisy
13. Wear comfortable, loose fitting, layered clothing to the testing center; prepare for it to be either cold or hot during the test
14. Bring at least 2 current forms of ID to the testing center
15. Arrive to the test early; be prepared to wait and be patient
16. Eliminate the obviously wrong answer choices, then guess the first remaining choice
17. Pace yourself; don't rush, but keep working and move on if you get stuck
18. Maintain a positive attitude even if the test is going poorly
19. Keep your first answer unless you are positive it is wrong
20. Check your work, don't make a careless mistake

Introduction to the TExES Series

Why am I required to take this TExES Assessment?

Your state requires you to take this TExES Assessment in order to test the breadth and depth of your knowledge in a specified subject matter. Texas has adopted the TExES series in order to ensure that you have mastered the subject matter you are planning to teach before they issue your teaching license.

Because the issuance of your license ensures competence in the subject area it is important that you take studying seriously and make sure you study thoroughly and completely.

Two Kinds of TExES Assessments

The TExES Series consist of two different kinds of assessments multiple-choice questions and constructed response test.

The multiple-choice test consists of questions followed by several answer choices. From these answer choices you select the answer that you think best corresponds with the given question. These questions can survey a wider range because they can ask more questions in a limited time period.

Constructed response questions consist of a given question for which you write an original response. These tests have fewer questions, but the questions require you to demonstrate the depth of you own personal knowledge in the subject area.

Reading and Understanding Text

Identifying and Interpreting Figurative Language and Other Literary Elements

You must be able to interpret and analyze the following:

Alliteration-use of the same consonant at the beginning of each stressed syllable in a line of verse

Example from *Hard Times* by Charles Dickens

I don't know what this - jolly old - Jaundiced Jail, Tom had paused to find a sufficiently complimentary and expressive name for the parental roof, and seemed to relieve his mind for a moment by the strong alliteration this one, 'would be without you.

Allusion-pointing to something from literature or history to express your point

Example:

He is Freudian if anything

Analogy

   a. Similarity in some respects between things that are otherwise dissimilar.
   b. A comparison based on such similarity.

Example:

Cats are like tigers.

Characterization- (through a character's words, thoughts, actions) the act or process of characterizing

Cliché- a trite or obvious remark

Examples:

Rome wasn't built in a day.

There are plenty more fish in the sea.

Dialect- the usage or vocabulary that is characteristic of a specific group of people

Example:

She has a strong German accent

Slang- characteristic language of a particular group (as among thieves)

Example:

They don't speak our language.

Figurative language- essential in certain types of writing to help convey meaning and expression. Figurative language is necessary to convey the exact meaning in a vivid and artistic manner, yet a concise and to the point manner to your reader. The writer has a story to tell and the language used must portray every emotion and feeling possible on the paper. If the writer does not create an image in the readers mind, he will lose the readers attention and holding the attention of the reader is the writer's goal.

Types of Figurative Language:

Simile- a comparison between two objects using the words "like" or "as."

Example:

Her voice is like a bird.

Metaphor- the comparison between two objects

Example:

His eyes are jewels.

Hyperbole- a very strong exaggeration

Example:

The teachers smile is as wide as the ocean.

Personification- gives an inhuman thing human quality

Example:

The diamonds are jealous of her beauty.

Foreshadowing- the act of providing vague advance indications; representing beforehand

Imagery-the ability to form mental images of things or events

Irony- incongruity between what might be expected and what actually occurs

Mood- a set of verb forms or inflections used to indicate the speaker's attitude toward the factuality or likelihood of the action or condition expressed. In English the indicative mood is used to make factual statements, the subjunctive mood to indicate doubt or unlikelihood, and the imperative mood to express a command

Point of view-a mental position from which things are viewed

Types of Point of Views:

   first-person- a character in the story who speaks in the first person voice

   third-person objective- a narrator, not a character in the story, who speaks in the third person voice and can tell only what is observable through the five senses

third-person omniscient- a narrator, not a character in the story, who speaks in the third person voice and can tell the thoughts and feelings of characters within the story

Setting- (established through description of scenes, colors, smells) the context and environment in which a story is set

Style- the way in which something is said, done, expressed, or performed

Symbolism- Symbol is a specific idea or object to represent ideas, values, or ways of life. A symbol is usually something more than what it seems

Tone- is the attitude of style or expression used to write

Voice- the grammatical relation (active or passive) of the grammatical subject of a verb to the action that the verb denotes

Identifying Patterns, Structures, and Characteristics of Literary Forms and Genres

Sonnet- a 14-line verse form usually having one of several conventional rhyme schemes

Haiku- a Japanese lyric verse form having three unrhymed lines of five, seven, and five syllables, traditionally invoking an aspect of nature or the seasons

Epic- an extended narrative poem in elevated or dignified language, celebrating the feats of a legendary or traditional hero

Free Verse- unrhymed verse without a consistent metrical pattern

Couplet-a unit of verse consisting of two successive lines, usually rhyming and having the same meter and often forming a complete thought or syntactic unit

Elegy-a mournful poem, lament for the dead

Limerick-a light humorous, nonsensical, or bawdy verse of five anapestic lines usually with the rhyme scheme *aabba*

Novel-a fictional prose narrative of considerable length, typically having a plot that is unfolded by the actions, speech, and thoughts of the characters

Short Story-a short piece of prose fiction, having few characters and aiming at unity of effect

Science Fiction-a literary or cinematic genre in which fantasy, typically based on speculative scientific discoveries or developments, environmental changes, space travel, or life on other planets, forms part of the plot or background

Fable-a usually short narrative making an edifying or cautionary point and often employing as characters animals that speak and act like humans

Myth-a traditional, typically ancient story dealing with supernatural beings, ancestors, or heroes that serves as a fundamental type in the worldview of a people, as by explaining aspects of the natural world or delineating the psychology, customs, or ideals of society

Legend- an unverified story handed down from earlier times, especially one popularly believed to be historical

Folk Tale-a story or legend forming part of an oral tradition

Fairy Tale- a fictional story involving humans, magical events, and usually animals. Characters such as fairies, elves, giants, and talking animals are taken from folklore. The plot often involves impossible events and/or an enchantment.

Mystery-a work of fiction, a drama, or a film dealing with a puzzling crime

Situating and Interpreting texts within their Historical and Cultural Context

Some of the Schools of Literature:

Harlem Renaissance- originally called the New Negro Movement; the Harlem Renaissance was a literary and intellectual flowering that fostered a new black cultural identity in the 1920s and 1930s

Authors include:

Langston Hughes, Countee Cullen, and Zora Neale Hurston

British Romantics- British literature and culture from roughly 1789–1832

Authors include:

Thomas Paine, Mary Wollstonecraft, Edmund Burke, William Blake, William Wordsworth, Anna Barbauld, Samuel Taylor Coleridge, Lord Byron, Percy Bysshe Shelley, John Keats, James Hogg and Thomas De Quincey. Secondary and critical texts will include readings from significant scholars and critics such as Jonathan Wordsworth, Susan Wolfson, David Bromwich, Anne Janowitz, Peter Garside and Jane Stabler

Metaphysical Poetry- is concerned with the whole experience of man, but the intelligence, learning and seriousness of the poets means that the poetry is about the profound areas of experience especially - about love, romantic and sensual; about man's relationship with God - the eternal perspective, and, to a less extent, about pleasure, learning and art

Authors include:

Andrew Marvell, George Herbert, and John Donne

Transcendentalism-a literary movement asserting the existence of an ideal spiritual reality that transcends the empirical and scientific and is knowable through intuition

Authors include:

Ralph Waldo Emerson, Henry David Thoreau, and Margaret Fuller

Identifying major works and authors of American, British, and World Literature from various cultures, genres, and periods

Some authors that you should be familiar with and an example of their work include:

Maya Angelou – *I Know Why the Caged Bird Sings*

Jane Austen- *Pride and Prejudice*

Ray Bradbury- *Fahrenheit 451*

Willa Cather- *My Antonia*

Stephen Crane- *The Red Badge of Courage*

Emily Dickinson- (poems) *Ascension*

Ralph Waldo Emerson-*Nature*

F. Scott Fitzgerald-*Great Gatsby*

Anne Frank- *The Diary of Anne Frank*

Robert Frost-*Stopping by the Woods on a Snowy Evening*

Zora Neale Hurston-Their Eyes Were Watching God

John Keats-Endymion

Harper Lee-To Kill a Mockingbird

C.S. Lewis- The Chronicles of Narnia

Herman Melville-*Moby Dick*

George Orwell-*1984*

Edgar Allan Poe- The Tell-Tale Heart

J.D. Salinger-Catcher in the Rye

William Shakespeare- *Romeo and Juliet*

Mary Shelley-*Frankenstein*

Percy Bysshe Shelley- *An Address, to the Irish People*

Amy Tan-*The Bonesetter's Daughter*

J.R.R. Tolkein-*The Hobbit*

Mark Twain- *Adventures of Huckleberry Finn*

Alice Walker-*Color Purple*

Walt Whitman-*Leaves of Grass*

Helpful Tips for Reading and Understanding Text

Skimming

Your first task when you begin reading is to answer the question "What is the topic of the selection?" This can best be answered by quickly skimming the passage for the general idea, stopping to read only the first sentence of each paragraph. A paragraph's first is usually the main topic sentence, and it gives you a summary of the content of the paragraph.

Once you've skimmed the passage, stopping to read only the first sentences, you will have a general idea about what it is about, as well as what is the expected topic in each paragraph.

Each question will contain clues as to where to find the answer in the passage. Do not just randomly search through the passage for the correct answer to each question. Search scientifically. Find key word(s) or ideas in the question that are going to either contain or be near the correct answer. These are typically nouns, verbs, numbers, or phrases in the question that will probably be duplicated in the passage. Once you have identified those key word(s) or idea, skim the passage quickly to find where those key word(s) or idea appears. The correct answer choice will be nearby.

Example: What caused Martin to suddenly return to Paris?

The key word is Paris. Skim the passage quickly to find where this word appears. The answer will be close by that word.

However, sometimes key words in the question are not repeated in the passage. In those cases, search for the general idea of the question.

Example: Which of the following was the psychological impact of the author's childhood upon the remainder of his life?

Key words are "childhood" or "psychology". While searching for those words, be alert for other words or phrases that have similar meaning, such as "emotional effect" or "mentally" which could be used in the passage, rather than the exact word "psychology".

Numbers or years can be particularly good key words to skim for, as they stand out from the rest of the text.

Example: Which of the following best describes the influence of Monet's work in the 20th century?

20th contains numbers and will easily stand out from the rest of the text. Use 20th as the key word to skim for in the passage.

Other good key word(s) may be in quotation marks. These identify a word or phrase that is copied directly from the passage. In those cases, the word(s) in quotation marks are exactly duplicated in the passage.

Example: In her college years, what was meant by Margaret's "drive for excellence"?

Paragraph Focus

Focus upon the first sentence of each paragraph, which is the most important. The main topic of the paragraph is usually there.

Once you've read the first sentence in the paragraph, you have a general idea about what each paragraph will be about. As you read the questions, try to determine which paragraph will have the answer. Paragraphs have a concise topic. The answer should either obviously be there or obviously not. It will save time if you can jump straight to the paragraph, so try to remember what you learned from the first sentences.

Example: The first paragraph is about poets; the second is about poetry. If a question asks about poetry, where will the answer be? The second paragraph.

The main idea of a passage is typically spread across all or most of its paragraphs. Whereas the main idea of a paragraph may be completely different than the main idea of the very next paragraph, a main idea for a passage affects all of the paragraphs in one form or another.

Example: What is the main idea of the passage?

For each answer choice, try to see how many paragraphs are related. It can help to count how many sentences are affected by each choice, but it is best to see how many paragraphs are affected by the choice. Typically the answer choices will include incorrect choices that are main ideas of individual paragraphs, but not the entire passage. That is why it is crucial to choose ideas that are supported by the most paragraphs possible.

Eliminate Choices

Some choices can quickly be eliminated. "Andy Warhol lived there." Is Andy Warhol even mentioned in the article? If not, quickly eliminate it.

When trying to answer a question such as "the passage indicates all of the following EXCEPT" quickly skim the paragraph searching for references to each choice. If the reference exists, scratch it off as a choice. Similar choices may be crossed off simultaneously if they are close enough.

In choices that ask you to choose "which answer choice does NOT describe?" or "all of the following answer choices are identifiable characteristics, EXCEPT which?" look for answers that are similarly worded. Since only one answer can be correct, if there are two answers that appear to mean the same thing, they must BOTH be incorrect, and can be eliminated.

Example:

A.)   changing values and attitudes

B.)   a large population of mobile or uprooted people

These answer choices are similar; they both describe a fluid culture. Because of their similarity, they can be linked together. Since the answer can have only one choice, they can also be eliminated together.

When presented with a question that offers two choices, or neither choice, or both choice, it is rarely both choices.

Example: When an atom emits a beta particle, the mass of the atom will:

A.   increase

B.   decrease.

C.   stay the same.

D.   either increase or decrease depending on conditions.

Answer D will rarely be correct, the answers are usually more concrete.

Contextual Clues

Look for contextual clues. An answer can be right but not correct. The contextual clues will help you find the answer that is most right and is correct. Understand the context in which a phrase is stated.

When asked for the implied meaning of a statement made in the passage, immediately go find the statement and read the context it was made in. Also, look for an answer choice that has a similar phrase to the statement in question. Example: In the passage, what is implied by the phrase "Churches have become more or less part of the furniture"?

Find an answer choice that is similar or describes the phrase "part of the furniture" as that is the key phrase in the question. "Part of the furniture" is a saying that means something is fixed, immovable, or set in their ways. Those are all similar ways of saying "part of the furniture." As such, the correct answer choice will probably include a similar rewording of the expression.

Example: Why was John described as "morally desperate".

The answer will probably have some sort of definition of morals in it. "Morals" refers to a code of right and wrong behavior, so the correct answer choice will likely have words that mean something like that.

"Drive for excellence" is a direct quote from the passage and should be easy to find.

Once you've quickly found the correct section of the passage to find the answer, focus upon the answer choices. Sometimes a choice will repeat word for word a portion of the passage near the answer. However, beware of such duplication – it may be a trap! More than likely, the correct choice will paraphrase or summarize the related portion of the passage, rather than being exactly the same wording.

For the answers that you think are correct, read them carefully and make sure that they answer the question. An answer can be factually correct, but it MUST answer the question asked. Additionally, two answers can both be seemingly correct, so be sure to read all of the answer choices, and make sure that you get the one that BEST answers the question.

Some questions will not have a key word.

Example: Which of the following would the author of this passage likely agree with?

In these cases, look for key words in the answer choices. Then skim the passage to find where the answer choice occurs. By skimming to find where to look, you can minimize the time required.

Sometimes it may be difficult to identify a good key word in the question to skim for in the passage. In those cases, look for a key word in one of the answer choices to skim for. Often the answer choices can all be found in the same paragraph, which can quickly narrow your search.

Fact/Opinion

When asked about which statement is a fact or opinion, remember that answer choices that are facts will typically have no ambiguous words. For example, how long is a long time? What defines an ordinary person? These ambiguous words of "long" and "ordinary" should not be in a factual statement. However, if all of the choices have ambiguous words, go to the context of the passage. Often a factual statement may be set out as a research finding.
Example: "The scientist found that the eye reacts quickly to change in light."

Opinions may be set out in the context of words like thought, believed, understood, or wished.

Example: "He thought the Yankees should win the World Series."

Opposites

Answer choices that are direct opposites are usually correct. The paragraph will often contain established relationships (when this goes up, that goes down). The question may ask you to draw conclusions for this and will give two similar answer choices that are opposites.

Example:

A.) if other factors are held constant, then increasing the interest rate will lead to a decrease in housing starts

B.) if other factors are held constant, then increasing the interest rate will lead to an increase in housing starts

Often these opposites will not be so clearly recognized. Don't be thrown off by different wording, look for the meaning beneath. Notice how these two answer choices are really opposites, with just a slight change in the wording shown above. Once you realize these are opposites, you should examine them closely. One of these two is likely to be the correct answer.

Example:

A.) if other factors are held constant, then increasing the interest rate will lead to a decrease in housing starts

B.) when there is an increase in housing starts, and other things remaining equal, it is often the result of an increase in interest rates

New Information

Correct answers will usually contain the information listed in the paragraph and question. Rarely will completely new information be inserted into a correct answer choice. Occasionally the new information may be related in a manner that the English Language, Literature, and Composition: Content Knowledge TExES is asking for you to interpret, but seldom.

Example:

The argument above is dependent upon which of the following assumptions?

A.) Scientists have used Charles's Law to interpret the relationship.

If Charles's Law is not mentioned at all in the referenced paragraph and argument, then it is unlikely that this choice is correct. All of the information needed to answer the question is provided for you, and so you should not have to make guesses that are unsupported or choose answer choices that have unknown information that cannot be reasoned.

Key Words

Look for answer choices that have the same key words in them as the question.

Example:

Which of the following, if true, would best explain the reluctance of politicians since 1980 to support this funding?

Look for the key words "since 1980" to be referenced in the correct answer choice. Most valid answer choices would probably include a phrase such as "since 1980, politicians have..."

Language and Linguistics

Understanding the principles of language acquisition and development, including social, cultural, and historical influences and the role of nature and dialects

This section focuses on how language skills develop, and influences on individuals' use of language. Once again understand the usage of dialects and the relationships between pronunciation and spelling. Know the phases of language development for secondary students learning English and strategies for building English Proficiency.

Understanding Elements of the History and Development of the English Language and American English

This section will test your knowledge and understanding of the history of the English language. Be familiar with the languages from which English is derived and modern languages from which English is related to. Also know the states of development of English and how languages can change over time.

Understand word etymologies (The origin and historical development of a linguistic form as shown by determining its basic elements, earliest known use, and changes in form and meaning, tracing its transmission from one language to another, identifying its cognates in other languages, and reconstructing its ancestral form where possible).

Understanding and Applying the elements of traditional grammar

Know and be able to identify the following:

Noun- the part of speech that is used to name a person, place, thing, quality, or action and can function as the subject or object of a verb, the object of a preposition, or an appositive

Proper Noun-a noun belonging to the class of words used as names for unique individuals, events, or places

Common Noun-a noun, such as book or dog, that can be preceded by the definite article and that represents one or all of the members of a class

Collective Noun-a noun that denotes a collection of persons or things regarded as a unit

Pronoun- the part of speech that substitutes for nouns or noun phrases and designates persons or things asked for, previously specified, or understood from the context

Verb- the part of speech that expresses existence, action, or occurrence in most languages

Adjective- the part of speech that modifies a noun or other substantive by limiting, qualifying, or specifying and distinguished in English morphologically by one of several suffixes, such as -able, -ous, -er, and -est, or syntactically by position directly preceding a noun or nominal phrase

Adverb- the part of speech that modifies a verb, adjective, or other adverb

Preposition- a word or phrase placed typically before a substantive and indicating the relation of that substantive to a verb, an adjective, or another substantive, as English at, by, with, from, and in regard to

Conjunction- the part of speech that serves to connect words, phrases, clauses, or sentences

Phrase-a sequence of words intending to have meaning

Appositive Phrase- an appositive is a re-naming or amplification of a word that immediately precedes it

Participial Phrase- includes the participle and the object of the participle or any words modified by or related to the participle

Prepositional Phrase- includes the preposition and the object of the preposition as well as any modifiers related to either

Clause- a group of related words that contain both a subject and a verb/predicate, thus it may be able to stand alone as a sentence

Independent Clause-a clause in a complex sentence that contains at least a subject and a verb and can stand alone syntactically as a complete sentence

Dependent Clause-a clause that cannot stand alone as a full sentence and functions as a noun, adjective, or adverb within a sentence

Syntactical Systems-

Subject-verb agreement- Singular subjects need singular verbs; plural subjects need plural verbs

Verb Tenses-

    present

    past

    perfect

    future

    future perfect

    Voice of verb-

        active

        passive

Pronoun-antecedent agreement and weak reference

Correct usage of infinitive and participle

Sentence Types-

    Declarative- used to form statements

    Interrogative-used to from questions

- 44 -

Exclamatory-used to express a strong feeling

Imperative-used to express or command

Sentence Structure-

Simple- contains only one clause

Compound-consist of two or more independent clauses joined by coordinating conjunctions

Complex- contains one independent clause and at least one dependent clause

Compound-complex-when a coordinating conjunction joins two complex sentences, or one simple sentence and one complex sentence

Understanding the elements of semantics and how these elements affect meaning

Understand how meaning is affected by punctuation or word order and how words can connote different things based on context. Know how euphemism (The act or an example of substituting a mild, indirect, or vague term for one considered harsh, blunt, or offensive) and other semantic strategies are used to obscure or alter meaning.

Composition and Rhetoric

Understanding and applying elements of teaching and writing

Know the stages of the writing process:

Prewriting- generate ideas for writing: brainstorming; reading literature; creating life maps, webs, and story charts; developing word banks; deciding on form, audience, voice, and purpose

Drafting- getting ideas on paper. They write without concern for conventions. Written work does not have to be neat

Revising- Improve what the narrative says and how it says it: write additions, imagery, and details. Take out unnecessary work. Use peer suggestions to improve

Editing- work together on editing for mechanics and spelling

Publishing - sending the work to publishers

Evaluating- final assessment on the work as a whole

Be familiar with different tools and response strategies for assessing student writing and when they should most appropriately be used.

      Conferencing

      Holistic Scoring

      Peer Reviews

      Portfolios

      Self-assessment

      Scoring rubrics

Understand common research and documentation techniques.

Using print and electronic media

Types of Reference Sources-

      Reference Works including encyclopedia, atlas, dictionary, etc.

      Internet like keyword searches, databases, indexes, bulletin boards

Other sources such as newspapers, journals, and magazines

Field Data such as surveys, questionnaires, field studies

Know criteria for evaluating source information such as:

Motives

Creditability

Perspectives

Date

Logic

Comprehensiveness of the evidence

Know times of bibliographical citations

MLA citations

APA citations

Understanding and Evaluating Rhetorical Features in Writing

Be able to evaluate a given passage of issues of audience and purpose as well as the organization, the creation, and preservation of coherence. You will be tested on you understanding of organizational and presentation strategies in print, electronic, and visual media.

Be familiar with the following organizational patterns:

Cause and Effect- one item is showed as having produced another element. An event (effect) is said to have happened because of some situation or circumstance (cause). The cause (the action) stimulates the event, or effect (the outcome)

Key words and phrases: for this reason, consequently, hence, because, on that account, made

Compare and Contrast- Items are related by the comparisons (similarities) that are made or by the contrasts (differences) that are presented. The author's purpose is to show similarities and differences

Keyword word and phrase-similar, different, bigger than, smaller than, parallels, however, but, on the other hand

Chronological (Time) Order or Sequence- Items are listed in the order in which they occurred or in a specifically planned order in which they must develop. In this case, the order is important and changing it would change the meaning

Compare and Contrast- similarities and differences between two subjects, consider how these will be presented

Spatial Sequence- Map ideas visually or literally with a visual aid

Problem and Solution- If you have a solution to present, first present the problem with a full description. Then follow this with a description of the solution and the methods employed to achieve this solution

Be familiar with graphs and charts including:

Bar graph- a graphical way of showing quantitative comparisons by using rectangular shapes with lengths proportional to the measure of what is being compared

Line graph- a diagram showing a system of connections or interrelations between two or more things by using lines

Pie Chart- a circular chart cut into segments illustrating relative magnitudes or frequencies

Be familiar with the typical organizational patterns used in the following:

> Textbooks
>
> Journal articles
>
> Newspaper Articles
>
> Television news programs

List the key aims and features of:

> Creative discourse
>
> Expository discourse
>
> Persuasive discourse

Be able to describe each of the following elements as a rhetorical strategy and make up some examples of each:

> Use of an analogy or extended metaphor
>
> Appeal to authority
>
> Appeal to emotion

Be able to recognize elements of style, tone, voice and point of view as part of rhetorical strategy, including sarcasm, criticism, and praise.

Be able to recognize bias, stereotypes, inferences, and assumptions and be able to distinguish between fact and opinion.

Social Studies

Geography

Longitude- Angular distance on the earth's surface, measured east or west from the prime meridian at Greenwich, England, to the meridian passing through a position, expressed in degrees (or hours), minutes, and seconds

Latitude- The angular distance north or south of the earth's equator, measured in degrees along a meridian, as on a map or globe

Equator- The imaginary great circle around the earth's surface, equidistant from the poles and perpendicular to the earth's axis of rotation. It divides the earth into the Northern Hemisphere and the Southern Hemisphere

International Dateline- An imaginary line on the surface of the earth following (approximately) the 180th meridian

Know the seven continents and their locations

Africa, Asia, Europe, Antarctica, North America, South America, and Australia

Know the four oceans

Indian Ocean, Pacific Ocean, Atlantic Ocean, and Artic Ocean

Know how to read a map and map legend. Be able to identify and interpret different kinds of maps. Know the kids of geographic features that make up the earth.

Weather- The state of the atmosphere at a given time and place, with respect to variables such as temperature, moisture, wind velocity, and barometric pressure

Climate- The meteorological conditions, including temperature, precipitation, and wind, that characteristically prevail in a particular region

Know how floods, droughts, earthquakes, erosion and snowstorms affect the Earth

Understand factors that affect settlement patterns and immigration. Know why some areas are sparsely populated while some areas are densely populated. Know immigration patterns and trends in the United States in the 19th and 20th centuries. Know the trends in the ethnic composition of the United States population.

International Organizations:

European Union (EU)- An economic and political union established in 1993 after the ratification of the Maastricht Treaty by members of the European Community, which forms its core. In establishing the European Union, the treaty expanded the political scope of the European Community, especially in the area of foreign and security policy, and provided for the creation of a central European bank and the adoption of a common currency by the end of the 20th century

World Trade Organization (WTO)- Administers the rules governing trade between its 144 Members. These rules help producers, exporters, and importers conduct their business, and ensure that trade flows as smoothly and predictably as possible. These rules also respect the right of governments to pursue broader goals such as sustainable development, the protection of human, animal or plant health, and the provision of public services

United Nations (UN)- An international organization composed of most of the countries of the world. It was founded in 1945 to promote peace, security, and economic development

North Atlantic Treaty Organization (NATO)- An international organization created in 1949 by the North Atlantic Treaty for purposes of collective security

Organization of Petroleum Exporting Countries (OPEC) – An organization of countries formed in 1961 to agree on a common policy for the sale of petroleum

Be able to comprehend the impact of the environment on human systems such as main essentials, transportation and recreation, and economic and industrial systems. Also know the effects of human initiated changes on the environment such as pollution, new construction, waste, global warming, ozone depletion. Understand what natural resources are and why they are important. Know what the ecosystem is and why it is important.

World History

Prehistoric and early Civilization

Paleolithic- of or relating to the cultural period of the Stone Age beginning with the earliest chipped stone tools, about 750,000 years ago, until the beginning of the Mesolithic Age, about 15,000 years ago. Also known as Old Stone Age.

Neolithic- of or relating to the cultural period of the Stone Age beginning around 10,000 B.C. in the Middle East and later elsewhere, characterized by the development of agriculture and the making of polished stone implements. Also known as New Stone Age

Know major characteristics of the following civilizations:

Mesopotamia (c. 3500-c. 2350 B.C.E.)

Indus River Valley (c. 2500- c. 1750 B.C.E.)

Early China (c. 1500-c. 771 B.C.E.)

Olmec society in Mesoamerica (c. 1200-c.400 B.C.E.)

Classic Civilizations

List the influences of geography on the civilization

Ancient Egypt (C. 2700-c. 1090 B.C.E.)

- Religious rulership
- Pyramids and the Valley of /kings
- Hieroglyphics and the Rosetta Stone

Greece (c. 2000-c. 300 B.C.E.)

- Mythology
- Social structure and the concepts of citizenship
- commerce, the city-state, and colonies
- Alexander the Great- king of Macedon; conqueror of Greece and Egypt and Persia; founder of Alexandria
- Athens
- Sparta

Rome (c. 700 B.C.E.- 500 C.E.)

- Mythology
- Military dominance
- Stages of government
- Origin and Spread of Christianity
- Constantinople
- Reason for the fall of the empire

Non-European Civilizations

India

- Caste system
- Hinduism- diverse body of religion, philosophy, and cultural practice native to and predominant in India, characterized by a belief in reincarnation and a supreme being of many forms and natures, by the view that opposing theories are aspects of one eternal truth, and by a desire for liberation from earthly evils
- Muslim conquest

Islam- a monotheistic religion characterized by the acceptance of the doctrine of submission to God and to Muhammad as the chief and last prophet of God

China

- Buddhism- the teaching of Buddha that life is permeated with suffering caused by desire, that suffering ceases when desire ceases, and that enlightenment obtained through right conduct, wisdom, and meditation releases one from desire, suffering, and rebirth
- Confucianism- of, relating to, or characteristic of Confucius, his teachings, or his followers
- Taoism- a principal philosophy and system of religion of China based on the teachings of Lao-tzu in the sixth century B.C. and on subsequent revelations. It advocates preserving and restoring the Tao in the body and the cosmos
- Construction of the Great Wall

Japan

- Feudalism- a political and economic system based on the holding of all land in fief or fee and the resulting relation of lord to vassal and characterized by homage, legal and military service of tenants, and forfeiture
- Shinotism- religion native to Japan, characterized by veneration of nature spirits and ancestors and by a lack of formal dogma

- Buddhism- see above
- Samurai, emperors, shoguns

Central and South America

- Mayas- a member of a Mesoamerican Indian people inhabiting southeast Mexico, Guatemala, and Belize, whose civilization reached its height around A.D. 300-900. The Maya are noted for their architecture and city planning, their mathematics and calendar, and their hieroglyphic writing system
- Aztecs- a member of a people of central Mexico whose civilization was at its height at the time of the Spanish conquest in the early 16th century
- Incas- a member of the group of Quechuan peoples of highland Peru who established an empire from northern Ecuador to central Chile before the Spanish conquest

Sub-Saharan African

- Trading empires
- Forest kingdoms

Rise and Expansion of Europe

- Feudalism- a political and economic system of Europe from the 9th to about the 15th century, based on the holding of all land in fief or fee and the resulting relation of lord to vassal and characterized by homage, legal and military service of tenants, and forfeiture
- The Black Death- the epidemic form of bubonic plague experienced during the Middle Ages when it killed nearly half the people of western Europe
- French Revolution- the revolution in France against the Bourbons; 1789-1799
- Napoleon Bonaparte- Emperor of the French (1804-1814). A brilliant military strategist, he deposed the French Directory (1799) and proclaimed

himself first consul and, later, emperor (1804). His military and political might gripped Continental Europe but failed to encompass Great Britain. After a disastrous winter campaign in Russia (1812), he was forced to abdicate (1814). Having been exiled to the island of Elba, he escaped, briefly regained power, and was ultimately defeated at Waterloo (1815) and exiled for life to the island of St. Helena. His codification of laws, the Napoleonic Code, still forms the basis of French civil law

- Industrial Revolution- The complex of radical socioeconomic changes, such as the ones that took place in England in the late 18th century, that are brought about when extensive mechanization of production systems results in a shift from home-based hand manufacturing to large-scale factory production
- Know the European colonies in Africa and Asia at the end of the 19th century
- Enlightenment
  - Locke
  - Rousseau
  - Jefferson
- Scientific Revolution
  - Newton- English mathematician and scientist who invented differential calculus and formulated the theory of universal gravitation, a theory about the nature of light, and three laws of motion. His treatise on gravitation, presented in *Principia Mathematica* (1687), was supposedly inspired by the sight of a falling apple
  - Galileo- Italian astronomer and mathematician; demonstrated that different weights descend at the same rate; perfected the refracting telescope that enabled him to make many discoveries (1564-1642)
  - Copernicus- Polish astronomer who advanced the theory that Earth and the other planets revolve around the sun, disrupting the Ptolemaic system of astronomy

- Reformation- A 16th-century movement in Western Europe that aimed at reforming some doctrines and practices of the Roman Catholic Church and resulted in the establishment of the Protestant churches
  - John Calvin
  - Martin Luther
- Renaissance- The humanistic revival of classical art, architecture, literature, and learning that originated in Italy in the 14th century and later spread throughout Europe
  - Da Vinci
  - Michelangelo
  - Machiavelli
- Know the voyages and conquest of the following:
  - Marco Polo- Venetian traveler who explored Asia from 1271 to 1295. His *Travels of Marco Polo* was the only account of the Far East available to Europeans until the 17th century
  - Christopher Columbus- Italian explorer in the service of Spain who determined that the earth was round and attempted to reach Asia by sailing west from Europe, thereby discovering America (1492). He made three subsequent voyages to the Caribbean in his quest for a sea route to China
  - Ferdinand Magellan- Portuguese navigator. While trying to find a western route to the Moluccas (1519), Magellan and his expedition were blown by storms into the strait that now bears his name (1520). He named and sailed across the Pacific Ocean, reaching the Marianas and the Philippines (1521), where he was killed fighting for a friendly native king. One of his ships returned to Spain (1522), thereby completing the first circumnavigation of the globe
  - Vasco da Gama- Portuguese explorer and colonial administrator. The first European to sail to India (1497-1498), he opened the rich lands of the East to Portuguese trade and colonization

20th Century Developments and Transformation

World War 1- a war between the allies (Russia, France, British Empire, Italy, United States, Japan, Rumania, Serbia, Belgium, Greece, Portugal, Montenegro) and the central powers (Germany, Austria-Hungary, Turkey, Bulgaria) from 1914 to 1918

Russian Revolution- the coup d'etat by the Bolsheviks under Lenin in November 1917 that led to a period of civil war which ended in victory for the Bolsheviks in 1922

Mexican Revolution- a Republic in southern North America; became independent from Spain in 1810

Chinese Revolution- the republican revolution against the Manchu dynasty in China; 1911-1912

Communism- A system of government in which the state plans and controls the economy and a single, often authoritarian party holds power, claiming to make progress toward a higher social order in which all goods are equally shared by the people

World War 2- a war between the Allies (Australia, Belgium, Bolivia, Brazil, Canada, China, Colombia, Costa Rica, Cuba, Czechoslovakia, Dominican Republic, El Salvador, Ethiopia, France, Greece, Guatemala, Haiti, Honduras, India, Iran, Iraq, Luxembourg, Mexico, Netherlands, New Zealand, Nicaragua, Norway, Panama, Philippines, Poland, South Africa, United Kingdom, United States, USSR, Yugoslavia) and the Axis (Albania, Bulgaria, Finland, Germany, Hungary, Italy, Japan, Rumania, Slovakia, Thailand) from 1939 to 1945

Holocaust- The genocide of European Jews and others by the Nazis during World War II: "Israel emerged from the Holocaust and is defined in relation to that catastrophe

Cold War- (c. 1945-1990) was the conflict between the two groups, loosely categorized as the *West* (the United States and its North Atlantic Treaty Organization (NATO) allies) and the *East* (the Soviet Union and its Warsaw Pact allies - loosely described as the Eastern Bloc). A full-scale "east versus west" war never actually broke out, hence the metaphor of a "cold" war with a predilection for quashing armed conflicts to prevent a "hot" and escalating shooting war whenever possible. Indeed, a good show was made on both sides that the conflict was primarily about economic, philosophic, cultural, social, and political ideology. The West criticized the East as embodying undemocratic totalitarianism and communist dictatorship while the East criticized the West as promoting bourgeois capitalism and imperialism. The attitude of both sides towards the other was summed up in the phrases used against each other; the East accused the West of promoting "middle class capitalism and imperialism that sidelined workers" while the West in the 1980s called the East the "evil empire" intent on subverting democracy for communist ideology

Lenin- Russian founder of the Bolsheviks, leader of the Russian Revolution (1917), and first head of the USSR (1917-1924). As a communist theoretician Lenin held that workers could not develop a revolutionary consciousness without the guidance of a vanguard party and that imperialism was a particular stage of capitalist development

Stalin- Soviet politician. The successor of Lenin, he was general secretary of the Communist Party (1922-1953) and premier (1941-1953) of the USSR. His rule was marked by the exile of Trotsky (1929), a purge of the government and military, the forced collectivization of agriculture, a policy of industrialization, and a victorious but devastating role for the Soviets in World War II

Mao Zedong- Chinese Communist leader and theorist. A founder of the Chinese Communist Party (1921), he led the Long March (1934-1935) and proclaimed the People's Republic of China in 1949. As party chairman and the country's first head of state (1949-1959) he initiated the Great Leap Forward and the founding of communes. He continued as party chairman after 1959 and was a leading figure in the Cultural Revolution (1966-1969). In the 1970s he consolidated his political power and established ties with the West

Mohandas Gandhi- Indian nationalist and spiritual leader who developed the practice of nonviolent disobedience that forced Great Britain to grant independence to India (1947). He was assassinated by a Hindu fanatic

Nelson Mandela- South African president (1994-1999) and Black political leader imprisoned for nearly 30 years for his anti-apartheid activities. Released in 1990, he led the African National Congress in negotiating an end to apartheid. In 1993 he shared the Nobel Peace Prize.

Post-Second World War decolinization in Africa and Asia and increased democracy in Europe, including:

- o India and Pakistan in 1947
- o Sub-Saharan nations in 1960s
- o Kenya, Angola, Mozabambique in the 1960's and 19+70's
- o Nations in Eastern Europe, the Balkans, and the former Soviet Union in the 1980's and 1990's
- o Fall of the Berlin Wall 1989

Know the rise of global culture and the rise of a global economy.

European Exploration and Colonization

Inuit- A member of a group of Eskimoan peoples inhabiting the Arctic from northern Alaska eastward to eastern Greenland, particularly those of Canada

Anasazi- A Native American culture flourishing in southern Colorado and Utah and northern New Mexico and Arizona from about A.D. 100, whose descendants are considered to include the present-day Pueblo people. Anasazi culture includes an early Basket Maker phase and a later Pueblo phase marked by the construction of cliff dwellings and by expert artisanship in weaving and pottery

Northwest Indians- A Native American people inhabiting parts of coastal British Columbia and northern Vancouver Island

Mound Builders- the tribe, or tribes, of North American aborigines who built, in former times, extensive mounds of earth, esp. in the valleys of the Mississippi and Ohio Rivers. Formerly they were supposed to have preceded the Indians, but later investigations go to show that they were, in general, identical with the tribes that occupied the country when discovered by Europeans

Iroquois- A Native American confederacy inhabiting New York State and originally composed of the Mohawk, Oneida, Onondaga, Cayuga, and Seneca peoples, known as the Five Nations. After 1722 the confederacy was joined by the Tuscaroras to form the Six Nations

Know and understand the interactions between the Native Americans and the Europeans. Understand colonial culture from different perspectives.

The American Revolution and the founding of the Nation

American Revolution- the revolution of the American colonies against Great Britain; 1775-1783

Declaration of Independence- the document recording the proclamation of the second Continental Congress (4 July 1776) asserting the independence of the colonies from Great Britain

Articles of Confederation- a written agreement ratified in 1781 by the thirteen original states; it provided a legal symbol of their union by gave the central government no coercive power over the states or their citizens

John Adams- The first Vice President (1789-1797) and second President (1797-1801) of the United States. He was a major figure during the American Revolution, the drafting of the Declaration of Independence, and the shaping of the Constitution

Thomas Jefferson- The third President of the United States (1801-1809). A member of the second Continental Congress, he drafted the Declaration of Independence (1776). His presidency was marked by the purchase of the Louisiana Territory from France (1803) and the Tripolitan War (1801-1805). A political philosopher, educator, and architect, Jefferson designed his own estate, Monticello, and buildings for the University of Virginia.

George Washington- American military leader and the first President of the United States (1789-1797). Commander of the American forces in the Revolutionary War (1775-1783), he presided over the Second Constitutional Convention (1787) and was elected President of the fledgling country (1789). He shunned partisan politics and in his farewell address (1796) warned against foreign involvement.

Benjamin Franklin - American public official, writer, scientist, and printer. After the success of his *Poor Richard's Almanac* (1732-1757), he entered politics and played a major part in the American Revolution. Franklin negotiated French support for the colonists, signed the Treaty of Paris (1783), and helped draft the Constitution

(1787-1789). His numerous scientific and practical innovations include the lightning rod, bifocal spectacles, and a stove

Constitution- The fundamental law of the United States, framed in 1787, ratified in 1789, and variously amended since then

Bill of Rights- The first ten amendments to the U.S. Constitution, added in 1791 to protect certain rights of citizens

Growth and Expansion of the Republic

Know the origins of slavery and how it is addressed in the US Constitution. Know about the acquisition of Florida, Oregon, Texas, and California

Louisiana Purchase- A territory of the western United States extending from the Mississippi River to the Rocky Mountains between the Gulf of Mexico and the Canadian border. It was purchased from France on April 30, 1803, for $15 million and officially explored by the Lewis and Clark expedition (1804-1806).

Manifest Destiny- The 19th-century doctrine that the United States had the right and duty to expand throughout the North American continent.

Mexican War- A war (1846-1848) between the United States and Mexico, resulting in the cession by Mexico of lands now constituting all or most of the states of California, Arizona, New Mexico, Nevada, Utah, and Colorado

War of 1812- a war (1812-1814) between the United States and England which was trying to interfere with American trade with France

Monroe Doctrine- an American foreign policy opposing interference in the Western hemisphere from outside powers

Trail of Tears - the illegal removal by the United States government of the Cherokee of Georgia to what was called Indian Territory in 1838-39. Several other of the five civilized tribes had their own versions of the Trail of Tears, which were also called as such

Eli Whitney- American inventor and manufacturer whose invention of the cotton gin (1793) revolutionized the cotton industry. He also established the first factory to assemble muskets with interchangeable parts, marking the advent of modern mass production

Civil War- The war in the United States between the Union and the Confederacy from 1861 to 1865.

Know the abolitionist movement, the women's movement, the Fugitive slave act, and Dred Scott case.

Abraham Lincoln- The 16th President of the United States (1861-1865), who led the Union during the Civil War and emancipated slaves in the South (1863). He was assassinated shortly after the end of the war by John Wilkes Booth

Harriet Tubman- American abolitionist. Born a slave on a Maryland plantation, she escaped to the North in 1849 and became the most renowned conductor on the Underground Railroad, leading more than 300 slaves to freedom

William Lloyd Garrison- American abolitionist leader who founded and published *The Liberator* (1831-1865), an antislavery journal

Harriet Beecher Stowe- American writer whose antislavery novel *Uncle Tom's Cabin* (1852) had great political influence and advanced the cause of abolition

Gettysburg Address- A 3-minute address by Abraham Lincoln during the American Civil War (November 19, 1863) at the dedication of a national cemetery on the site of the Battle of Gettysburg

Emancipation Proclamation- An order issued during the Civil War by President Lincoln ending slavery in the Confederate states

Andrew Carnegie- Scottish-born American industrialist and philanthropist who amassed a fortune in the steel industry and donated millions of dollars for the benefit of the public

John D. Rockefeller- United States industrialist who made a fortune in the oil business and gave half of it away (1839-1937

Panama canal- a ship canal 40 miles long across the Isthmus of Panama built by the United States (1904-1914)

20th Century Developments and Transformations

Harlem Renaissance- originally called the New Negro Movement; the Harlem Renaissance was a literary and intellectual flowering that fostered a new black cultural identity in the 1920s and 1930s

Authors include:

Langston Hughes, Countee Cullen, and Zora Neale Hurston

Prohibition- a law forbidding the sale of alcoholic beverages; "in 1920 the 18th amendment to the Constitution established prohibition in the US"

Women's Suffrage- The movement for Women's suffrage, led by suffragists and suffragettes, was a social, economic and political reform movement aimed at extending equal suffrage, the right to vote to women, according to the one-man-one-vote principle.

The Great Depression- a time period during the 1930s when there was a worldwide economic depression and mass unemployment

The New Deal- The programs and policies to promote economic recovery and social reform introduced during the 1930s by President Franklin D. Roosevelt

Korean War- A conflict that lasted from 1950 to 1953 between North Korea, aided by China, and South Korea, aided by United Nations forces consisting primarily of U.S. troops

McCarthyism- The practice of publicizing accusations of political disloyalty or subversion with insufficient regard to evidence

The Decisions to drop atomic bombs on Nagasaki and Hiroshima

Desegregation- To open (a school or workplace, for example) to members of all races or ethnic groups, especially by force of law

Vietnam War- a protracted military conflict (1954-1975) between the Communist forces of North Vietnam supported by China and the Soviet Union and the non-Communist forces of South Vietnam supported by the United States.

Understand the rise of the consumer oriented society and changing demographic populations and how they play a role in society. Also understand the role of the development of computers and information technology.

Government and Civics

Nature and Purpose of Government

Government- The act or process of governing, especially the control and administration of public policy in a political unit

Government serves many purposes including: collective decision making and conflict resolution

Forms of Government

There are several forms of Government including:

Federalism

Parliamentary system

Constitutional structures

Unitary systems

United States Constitution

Separation of power between three branches of government:

Legislative Branch- made up of the Congress and government agencies, such as the Government Printing Office and Library of Congress that provide assistance to and support services for the Congress. Article I of the Constitution established this branch and gave Congress the power to make laws. Congress has two parts, the House of Representatives and the Senate

Judicial Branch- made up of the court system. The Supreme Court is the highest court in the land. Article III of the Constitution established this Court and all other Federal courts were created by Congress. Courts decide arguments about the meaning of laws, how they are applied, and whether they break the rules of the Constitution.

Executive Branch- makes sure that the laws of the United States are obeyed. The President of the United States is the head of the executive branch of government. This branch is very large so the President gets help from the Vice President, department heads (Cabinet members), and heads of independent agencies

Rights and Responsibilities of Citizens

US citizens have Freedom of speech, press, assembly, petition, religion, and privacy. We also have property rights, the right to choose one's work, the right to join or not join a labor union, and the right to apply for copyrights and patents

There are also legal obligations to abide by such as obey the law, pay taxes, and serve on jury.

Understand the process immigrants go through to become a US citizen.

Know Landmark Supreme Court Decisions such as:

Roe vs. Wade

Marbury vs. Madison

Plessy vs. Ferguson

Miranda vs. Arizona

Brown vs. Board of Education

State and Local Government

Know responsibilities of state and local government and the relationship between state government and federal government.

Behavioral Sciences (Anthropology, Sociology, and Psychology)

Anthropology

Anthropology- The scientific study of the origin, the behavior, and the physical, social, and cultural development of humans

Archaeology- The systematic study of past human life and culture by the recovery and examination of remaining material evidence, such as graves, buildings, tools, and pottery

Know how family patterns address basic human needs. Understand how human experience and cultural expression contribute to the development and transmission of culture.

Sociology

Sociology- The study of human social behavior, especially the study of the origins, organization, institutions, and development of human society

Understand the role of socialization in society and the effects that it has.

Social stratification- the condition of being arranged in social strata or classes

Social mobility- The movement or shifting of membership between or within social classes by individuals or by groups

Understand the terms stereotypes, bias, values, and ideals.

Psychology

Psychology- The science that deals with mental processes and behavior

Know the following terms:

Behavioralism

Cognitive development

Character

Emotions

Physiological influences

Social Influences

Needs vs. Wants

Perception

Motives

Values

Individual

Learning

Human development and growth is broken into four stages: infancy, childhood, adolescence, and adulthood. Also know about gender influences

Economics

The Market

Scarcity- Insufficiency of amount or supply; shortage

Cost- An amount paid or required in payment for a purchase

Resources- Something that can be used for support or help

Needs- A condition or situation in which something is required

Wants- To desire greatly; wish for

Opportunity Cost- cost in terms of foregone alternatives

Market- The business of buying and selling a specified commodity

Property- Something owned; a possession

Capital- Wealth in the form of money or property, used or accumulated in a business by a person, partnership, or corporation

Price- The amount as of money or goods, asked for or given in exchange for something else

Competition- Rivalry between two or more businesses striving for the same customer or market

Supply- the amount at which a producer is willing and able to produce

Demand-the amount at which a buyer is willing and able to buy

Production- The act or process of producing

Consumption- The act or process of consuming

Inflation- A persistent increase in the level of consumer prices or a persistent decline in the purchasing power of money, caused by an increase in available currency and credit beyond the proportion of available goods and services

Recession- An extended decline in general business activity, typically three consecutive quarters of falling real gross national product

Trade- The business of buying and selling commodities; commerce

Know the following institutions:

Labor unions

Corporation

Banks

Insurance Companies

Nonprofit institutions

Individuals and the Market

Employment- The work in which one is engaged; occupation

Unemployment- Out of work, especially involuntarily; jobless

Minimum Wage- The lowest wage, determined by law or contract that an employer may pay an employee for a specified job

Cost of living- The average cost of the basic necessities of life, such as food, shelter, and clothing

Know different types of marketing such as public relations, advertising, and customer service.

Be familiar with skills that good workers must possess.

Economics' effect of Population and Resources

Understand what natural, capital, and human resources are. Know what is meant by division of labor.

Government's role in economics and economics' impact on government

Know reasons why governments levy taxes such as military salaries, roads, schools, know the Government's role in maintaining the currency.

Federal Reserve- the central bank of the US; incorporates 12 Federal Reserve branch banks and all national banks and stated charted commercial banks and some trust companies

Consumer Price Index- An index of prices used to measure the change in the cost of basic goods and services in comparison with a fixed base period

Gross National Product- The total market value of all the goods and services produced by a nation during a specified period

Gross Domestic Product- The total market value of all the goods and services produced within the borders of a nation during a specified period

Economic Systems

Know the characteristics of the following:

Socialism

Capitalism

Communism

Command economies

Traditional economies

Free-market economies

International Economies

Imports- To bring or carry in from an outside source, especially to bring in (goods or materials) from a foreign country for trade or sale

Exports- To send or transport (a commodity, for example) abroad, especially for trade or sale

Tariffs- A list or system of duties imposed by a government on imported or exported goods

Quotas- A proportional share, as of goods, assigned to a group or to each member of a group; an allotment

Economics sanctions- Restrictions upon international trade and finance that one country imposes on another for political reasons.

Exchange rate- the charge for exchanging currency of one country for currency of another

Practice Test

Practice Questions

1. A teacher instructs a student to read a passage from a novel aloud. The teacher is assessing the student's ability to:

    a. read aloud with proper tone and inflection.

    b. master public speaking.

    c. decode words.

    d. pronounce words.

2. Supporters of word recognition instruction believe that:

    a. words should be taught in isolation.

    b. words should be taught both in isolation and in context.

    c. words should be taught in context.

    d. words should be taught orally only.

3. An 8th grade teacher uses round robin or "popcorn" reading during the <u>Diary of Anne Frank</u> unit. She then questions students extensively about characters' feelings and motivations, being careful not to ask yes/no questions. This demonstrates her understanding of how students acquire:

    a. reading proficiency.

    b. vocabulary.

    c. written language.

    d. syntax.

4. A 4th grade teacher creates an interdisciplinary unit about folk tales, fairy tales, and children's literature from around the world. Students are encouraged to study

and acquire foreign language vocabulary, as well as the backgrounds of different authors and cultural mores. This unit helps students improve oral language development by:

    a. increasing vocabulary

    b. improving fluency

    c. improving self-esteem

    d. building on home backgrounds and cultures

5. Reading aloud, or oral reading, primarily develops students':

    a. decontextualized language.

    b. vocabulary.

    c. listening skills.

    d. writing skills.

6. A 4th grade class has just completed a six-week unit on rainforest inhabitants. They begin reading a short story about a student who actively tries to save the rainforest. Alan, a student in the class, cannot answer several previewing questions because he cannot understand the questions or remember vocabulary being repeated from the previous unit. He is unable to:

    a. set a purpose for his reading.

    b. recall prior knowledge.

    c. understand different ways of reading.

    d. read.

7. Despite numerous interventions involving parents, Alan has not shown any improvement in his ability to acquire and use new vocabulary. The next step should be:

    a. more interventions.

    b. forcing him to read more.

    c. referral to a reading specialist for testing.

d. immediate placement in the lowest-level reading circle.

8. Ms. Jones has suggested to her 4th grade reading students that they find ways to personalize meaning in what they are reading. Which of the following would *best* help a group of emergent readers?

    a. memorization

    b. poetry

    c. mnemonic devices

    d. songs

9. A 5th grade student has been evaluated due to a reading deficiency. It is determined that the student is retelling the story based on pictures or classmates' participation and responses. Based on this information, the student is in which stage of reading development?

    a. 3

    b. 2

    c. 1

    d. 0

10. A 4th grade student is in stage 3 of reading development. This means she is ready to:

    a. read for knowledge and learning.

    b. read chapter books.

    c. begin learning a foreign language.

    d. become a peer tutor.

11. Children who do not have solid decoding skills cannot improve vocabulary through reading a variety of materials because they cannot:

    a. read.

    b. recognize unknown words or use context clues.

c. understand formal writing.

d. understand newspapers.

12. Which of the following strategies would *best* improve high-frequency word recognition?

a. word walls

b. flash cards

c. repeated reading of words in context or short phrases

d. word banks

13. The greatest gain in reading skills will occur when the material's difficulty is at the student's:

a. grade level.

b. instructional level.

c. chronological age level.

d. classmates' level.

14. A 6th grade teacher is implementing paired reading in her classroom. When she selects reading materials for the different groups, she should assign readings from texts in which students have:

a. 90-95% accuracy in word recognition.

b. 70-75% accuracy in word recognition.

c. 75-80% accuracy in word recognition.

d. 80-85% accuracy in word recognition.

15. A teacher is reading one-on-one with a 4th grade student who struggles with decoding. The teacher is attempting to use structural cues to help the student, which means she is using:

a. alphabetic principle.

b. prefixes, suffixes, roots.

c. syntax.

d. semantics.

16. Mr. Fox is using both paired and silent reading in his middle school reading class. He has a wide range of abilities in the classroom, from ESOL to special education. How can he best guide the students' selection of independent reading materials?

    a. Randomly assign books.

    b. Offer books/materials that he assumes they would like.

    c. Allow their friends to recommend reading.

    d. Conduct student interest surveys and allow students to choose materials that focus on their areas of interest.

17. Ms. Stone is teaching an elementary school reading unit on interpreting information from maps, graphs, etc. With what materials can she best help teach students how to locate, retrieve, and retain information?

    a. Current events texts such as newspapers and magazines

    b. Textbooks

    c. Pamphlets

    d. Novels or reading texts

18. Mr. Smith frequently assesses writing in his 8th grade language arts classes. What is the *best* way to assess students' skills and demonstrate their understanding of conventions of writing?

    a. Always assess all students on each convention.

    b. Assess students separately on conventions, content, and ideas over a period of time.

    c. Assess only on content.

    d. Assess only on grammar.

19. How would a diverse group of secondary students (grades 7-8, specifically) *best* develop proficiency in applying writing conventions?

    a. Write paragraphs on assigned topics.

    b. With partners, write creative writing pieces.

    c. In small groups, write factual essays.

    d. Both individually and in pairs, practice writing in a variety of genres on a variety of topics.

20. A middle school language arts teacher has given her students a choice in their culminating unit assessment. They may create a small newspaper with the requisite sections (i.e., editorial, metro, sports), or they may write a play or short story. All assignments must involve the unit themes and vocabulary. This assignment best demonstrates the teacher's ability to:

    a. incorporate technology.

    b. provide opportunities for revision.

    c. provide opportunities to write for various audiences, purposes, and settings.

    d. apply good instructional practices.

21. An upper elementary teacher is currently planning a Holocaust unit. She is trying to decide which ancillary and media materials she will use. Which of the following would create the best learning opportunities for her students?

    a. Newspaper articles from that time period

    b. Interviews

    c. Documentaries, political cartoons, video and voice recorded interviews, as well as written media

    d. Autobiographical books

22. A 7th grade teacher is planning activities to coincide with field trips to both the "Newseum" and the Holocaust Museum in Washington, D.C. Before the trip, he:

    • engages students in a journalism unit on TV and newsmagazines.

- provides students with a "scavenger hunt" list of items and ideas to find in the museums.
- holds whole-class discussions regarding current events.

Which of the following should he do after the field trip to help students analyze visual makers' choices?

a. Each student creates his or her own current events exhibit.

b. Students write an essay about their experience.

c. Students write their own newspaper.

d. Students write their own news articles and broadcast in pairs.

23. A 7th grade teacher is preparing to start a novel study using a book whose protagonist is a scientist. The novel has unusual themes and science-specific vocabulary. The teacher feels it will be a great opportunity for the students. How can she best preview this lesson and novel study?

a. Introduce new vocabulary and science concepts using manipulatives and real life examples.

b. Have students read a newspaper article about the author.

c. Have students read the pertinent chapters in their science text.

d. Have students read Chapter 1 and answer questions.

24. The Texas Essential Knowledge and Skills (TEKS) states that 6th grade students should be able to "use graphic sources of information to address research questions." Therefore, students should:

a. create charts or tables that summarize information.

b. summarize information on graphic organizers.

c. correctly copy teacher-generated charts, etc.

d. correctly use an encyclopedia or reference book.

25. At the end of a Holocaust unit focusing on Anne Frank, an 8th grade teacher assigns students the task of packing a suitcase so as to simulate the act of going into hiding. By doing so, they are able to demonstrate what is most important to them. She supplies them with a rubric and general instructions. She is providing students with:

    a. tedious tasks.

    b. boring assignments.

    c. difficult assessments.

    d. meaningful instruction.

26. Which of the following must a student have in order to move on to reading for meaning?

    a. Rapid word recognition

    b. Paired reading

    c. Round robin reading

    d. Decoding skills

Questions 27 to 30 pertain to the following passage used in an 8th grade reading class:

    Harper Smith could never have predicted that she would have her epiphany at a Saks makeup counter. The psychic in Sedona had warned her, had predicted she would "reveal herself under the watchful eye of another," but Harper didn't think that meant a perky salesgirl trying to sell her charcoal eyeliner. The girl applied it swiftly to her lids, and Harper peeked in the mirror. She had to admit to herself that it *did* look good; her eyes were dark blue and had a smoky tint that made them look almost purple. Every time she came to this counter they tried to convince her to buy the dark gray or the sparkly green shadow to complement her eyes. But every time she bought makeup and applied it at home, she never looked the same as she did in the store, which in her opinion was one of life's great inequities.

27. A student asks his reading partner the definition of "epiphany". The student responds that he does not know for sure, but assumes that it is a realization. The reading partner is using which of the following to help his classmate?

    a. Context clues

    b. Teacher direction

    c. Dictionary

    d. Thesaurus

28. Susan, a top reading student, is excited by this passage and tells the class of a time when she also had a life-changing realization. Another less-gifted student recounts a time she went shopping at the makeup counter with her mother. This gets the class interested mostly because the teacher is allowing:

    a. discussion.

    b. group work.

    c. real-life anecdotes or examples.

    d. book assignments.

29. Ms. Smith, the teacher, asks students to form a character analysis about Harper Smith from this very short passage. Most of the students are at Stage 2 or 3 of reading development and are able to tell her that Harper is:

    a. shy.

    b. stubborn.

    c. lacking in self-esteem.

    d. artistic.

30. Ms. Smith also has the students act out this scene, an activity known as reader's theater. Reader's theater is an effective and authentic way to:

    a. determine the best actors in the class.

    b. determine who is the best reader in the class.

    c. communicate meaning.

d. learn new acting methods.

31. Oral support reading, or OSR, requires students to follow along silently while listening to the text orally. This activity *best* reinforces:

    a. recognition of words and phrases.

    b. decontextualizing.

    c. literacy circles.

    d. vocabulary acquisition.

32. While Fast Start is a program designed for students in kindergarten through 2nd grade, it can also be effective for 4th or even 5th grade students. Parents are asked to help with Fast Start by spending _____ every day implementing the program with their children.

    a. 30 minutes

    b. 50 minutes

    c. 15 minutes

    d. 45 minutes

33. Poetry is also an extremely effective means of improving reading *mostly* because poems contain such a variety of:

    a. skills.

    b. topics.

    c. words.

    d. literary devices.

34. Not only does oral reading build fluency, it also builds or supports:

    a. meekness.

    b. confidence.

    c. poor behavior.

    d. intelligence.

35. In our current global economy and society, students need to be able to quickly bookmark and retrieve data from a variety of materials. This is most significant because the majority of research is now completed using:

   a. textbooks.

   b. encyclopedias.

   c. dictionaries.

   d. the Internet.

36. For middle grades students, it is important to model good word-learning behaviors. This includes:

   a. having students read selected texts with no prior assistance.

   b. giving students the definition to every word they do not know.

   c. providing students with hardcover or online dictionaries.

   d. previewing vocabulary prior to reading and semantic maps.

37. Acrostic poems and Venn diagrams are both examples of:

   a. webs.

   b. graphic organizers.

   c. group work.

   d. teacher-led instruction.

Questions 38 to 44 pertain to the following passage (a continuation of the previous passage from an 8th grade class):

> It was now that Harper had her realization, as she vacillated between eye shadows to wear to Randall's birthday party tonight. Nothing looked right to her, and everything seemed to be clouded with that patina of awkwardness. Her clothes, although fashionable, always to her looked dowdy and drab; the smoothies at the neighborhood juice bar looked fresh and stylish in the other patrons' hands, but in hers felt supersized and too

sugary. But now, under the hopeful eye of the clerk and with shocking clarity, Harper realized why nothing in her life felt right. She sucked in her breath and, in her childhood gesture of comfort, tugged at errant pieces of hair that had escaped from her ponytail. Her chestnut colored hair curled in the shape of corkscrews and was a lovely contrast to her ivory skin. Yet the rest of her family had straight black hair that seemed immune to the effects of humidity and warm olive complexions. Even in the midst of her revelation she silently cursed herself for inheriting the recessive traits from her grandmother.

38. A student has just read the above passage and does not understand the word "patina." The teacher should do which of the following to help the student?

   a. Encourage him to use context clues and prior knowledge.

   b. Tell him the answer.

   c. Tell him to look in the dictionary.

   d. Tell him to ask a classmate.

39. Another student in the same class reads the same passage from above. She is able to figure out the meaning of "patina" without asking the teacher for assistance and continues reading. She is in which stage of reading?

   a. 0

   b. 1

   c. 2

   d. 3

40. One student in this same class cannot figure out why the passage includes higher-order thinking words such as "patina" or "vacillate." The teacher can best explain the author's methods by pointing to:

   a. proper grammar.

   b. last week's vocabulary lesson.

c. author's purpose and audience writing.

d. Middle English.

41. The teacher asks her students to list out all the context clues or words that will indicate that "errant" is in fact a word for "astray". One student lists the word "makeup". His answer should provide which of the following for the teacher?

    a. A short timeout in which she explains why he is wrong

    b. Evidence of the need for referral to the reading specialist

    c. A parent conference

    d. Removal of the student from class

42. As part of the reading comprehension questions, the teacher asks the students to compare Harper's experience with a time during which they also felt awkward or had a realization. She is calling upon their _____ to make the comparison:

    a. textbook knowledge

    b. extra credit

    c. personal experience and prior knowledge

    d. friend's answers

43. The teacher would like to emphasize the fact that the passage is targeting a specific group of readers. Which of the following ideas best applies here?

    a. Writing for an audience

    b. Setting

    c. Vernacular

    d. Syntax

44. Based on the reading, what would be a synonym for "vacillate"?

    a. flat

    b. indecisive

    c. special

d. choice

45. A child in the class is in stage 3 of reading development, and the teacher believes him to be on the cusp of reaching stage 4. Once he reaches that stage, he will now be able to:

    a. decode words.

    b. read chapter books.

    c. understand relationships and viewpoints in fiction and non-fiction writing.

    d. help his peers decode the text.

46. The teacher asks the class to role play a situation in which they have to sell a product to a reluctant customer. This will engage the students because it uses:

    a. role play

    b. personal knowledge

    c. interesting assignments

    d. vocabulary

47. The teacher asks students to infer Harper's age from the passage. Many students say that Harper is an adult, based on the fact that she is shopping alone. This lesson is an example of:

    a. the emerging stage of readers.

    b. the importance of author's word choice.

    c. character formation.

    d. character relationships.

48. During a unit in which students read The BFG, students learned that words often have different meanings. This will help students understand that words do not exist in a vacuum; in fact, it will help them use words:

    a. in their homework assignments.

    b. in this novel study.

c. in a variety of contexts.

d. in stereotypical contexts.

49. As students enter the higher stages of reading development, as well as the upper-middle school years, they should begin to realize that learning vocabulary does not just mean learning synonyms. An effective reading or language arts teacher should teach these students:

a. how language gives meaning.

b. that words should be retained only for the assessments.

c. higher-level synonyms.

d. the same vocabulary words in a foreign language.

50. It is crucial for students to be part of an environment rich in verbal skills. One way to promote this environment is to:

a. encourage students to read the dictionary.

b. encourage students to read a variety of materials.

c. encourage students to read every night.

d. encourage students to recognize words from school lessons in the outside world.

51. In the Louisiana Purchase, the U.S. doubled its land area by purchasing land from France for:

a. $15 million

b. $30 million

c. $25 million

d. $10 million

52. In the early to mid 19th century, many eastern Indian tribes were forced west under the belief of:

a. slavery.

b. expanding state governments.

c. Manifest Destiny.

d. statutory law.

53. The Compromise of 1850 allowed California to enter the Union as a free state. This compromise was reached after the U.S. gained this land in the:

a. Louisiana Purchase.

b. Civil War.

c. War of 1812.

d. Mexican War.

54. One reason the Compromise of 1850 failed was because Kansas and what other state were created by Congress is 1854?

a. Missouri

b. Nebraska

c. Georgia

d. North Dakota

55. Which of the following groups rushed to Kansas to settle and fight for control of the territory in the 1850s?

a. Whigs and Republicans

b. Suffragists and businessmen

c. Abolitionists and slave owners

d. Democrats and farmers

56. In the Dred Scott decision of 1857, the court denied Mr. Scott his right to:

a. freedom.

b. sue.

c. vote.

d. pay taxes.

57. During the Civil War, Delaware, Kentucky, Maryland, and Missouri were labeled as "border starts" because they:

    a. bordered slave states.

    b. bordered each other.

    c. bordered bodies of water.

    d. bordered free states.

58. One *major* economic issue during Reconstruction was that the majority of land owners (black and white) could not afford to own their own land. This was caused primarily by:

    a. having to pay taxes and not having labor to work the land.

    b. the presence of scalawags.

    c. the Freedmen's Bureau.

    d. land destruction.

59. During Reconstruction, carpetbaggers could be compared to:

    a. busy bees.

    b. shy and meek turtles.

    c. vultures feasting on prey.

    d. helpful work horses or mules.

60. Absolute location is defined as:

    a. position of one place in relation to another.

    b. the exact spot on the earth's surface where a place is found.

    c. cardinal directions.

    d. intermediate directions.

61. One way geography affects our lives is in our jobs. For example, the mountains in Colorado created a huge mining industry. This demonstrates how _____ affect our culture.

    a. erosion

    b. weathering

    c. location

    d. landforms

62. Mountains are often formed when two _____ collide.

    a. pieces of magma or lava

    b. continental plates

    c. layers of Earth

    d. continents

63. Geographers study the world's main financial centers, such as London or New York, to best ascertain which of the following?

    a. How the economy affects the world.

    b. How London's economy affects England.

    c. How New York's economy affects the United States.

    d. How the world affects specific city economies.

64. Both _____ and _____ are leading causes of erosion of landforms.

    a. wind, glaciers

    b. westerlies, trade winds

    c. volcanoes, water

    d. sun, snow

65. Prevailing winds are defined as:

    a. the place were two air masses of different temperature meet.

    b. a region's average weather conditions.

c. winds that blow in the same direction over large areas of Earth.

d. short-term changes in air.

66. Tundras are almost always found in:

a. coasts in low longitudes.

b. coasts in high longitudes.

c. coasts in low latitudes.

d. coasts in high latitudes.

67. A command economy differs from a market economy in that:

a. a command economy is based on free trade.

b. a command economy is a productive economy.

c. a command economy is completely controlled by the central government.

d. a command economy is stagnant.

68. The advent of the first national highway in 1818 was in direct response to the growth of America's population because:

a. new political parties demanded the road.

b. people were tired of shipping.

c. roads were needed for settlers' travel and crop transportation.

d. it was part of Reconstruction.

69. Railroads became the economically smartest and most efficient way to transport people and goods. This inexpensive form of transportation was first seen in:

a. France

b. England

c. Germany

d. Ireland

70. Which of the following is the best example of a command economy?

a. India

b. China

c. Egypt

d. United States

71. The free enterprise system is based on the four basic principles of private property rights, profit motive of owners, freedom of choice, and:

a. owner control.

b. federal government control.

c. local government control.

d. state government control.

72. The current economic recession has affected supply and demand in several ways. For example, unemployment leads to more supply than demand because it:

a. helps investors gain value.

b. is an example of a drop in business activity.

c. affects the amount of goods and services that consumers are willing and able to buy.

d. puts financial or legal limitations on trade.

73. A mixed economy can be defined as:

a. a system based on private ownership.

b. synonymous with command economy.

c. a combination of traditional, command, and market economies.

d. a system based on customs.

74. The automobile industry is a good example of:

a. a communist market.

b. interdependence.

c. a free market.

d. recession.

75. Henry Ford's assembly line revolutionized factory production in the early 20th century. However, one *negative* impact of the assembly line on workers was that it:

    a. decreased the selection or variety of goods.

    b. increased manager satisfaction.

    c. increased worker satisfaction.

    d. decreased the importance of independence.

76. The presidential veto power is an example of:

    a. federalism.

    b. bicameral legislation.

    c. checks and balances.

    d. the executive branch.

77. The quote, "No person shall be deprived of life, liberty, or property except by due process of law." is from which document?

    a. The Articles of Confederation

    b. The United States Constitution

    c. The Texas State Constitution

    d. The Bill of Rights

78. In order to amend the United States Constitution, ___ of each House must propose the amendment, and _____ of the states must ratify it.

    a. 1/3, 3/4

    b. 3/4, 1/3

    c. 2/3, 3/4

    d. 3/4, 2/3

79. The Civil War greatly changed Federalism by:

a. changing the idea that state and national governments were equal powers.

b. giving states more power.

c. allowing states to secede.

d. ratifying state constitutions.

80. The Sherman Anti-Trust Act was created mostly by actions of:

a. the federal government.

b. railroads and corporations.

c. small businesses.

d. politicians.

81. In Brown v. Board of Education, the court decided *against*:

a. segregation.

b. desegregation.

c. the right to public education.

d. charter schools.

82. The Civil Rights Act of 1964 and the Voting Rights Act of 1965 increased _____ over actions normally handled by states.

a. presidential veto

b. Congressional power

c. federal authority

d. state power

83. A slight power shift occurred after the Great Depression during the New Deal because when states accepted federal funds:

a. they were free to spend the monies however they saw fit.

b. they were given more voting power.

c. they had to accept attached federal regulations.

d. they were given more seats in the House and Senate.

84. The primary effect of the Bill of Rights has been:

a. to increase executive branch power.

b. to secure the effectiveness of checks and balances.

c. to clarify the Constitution's language.

d. to increase the democracy contained in the Constitution.

85. What is the *most* significant consequence of the Supreme Court's ruling in Marbury v. Madison?

a. It established "separate but equal" doctrine.

b. It established judicial review.

c. It established constitutional supremacy.

d. It gave more power to states.

86. The biggest cultural difference between the U.S. and India is:

a. the presence of democracy in the United States.

b. the presence of the caste system in India.

c. the presence of extreme poverty in India.

d. the presence of the Constitution in the United States.

87. One major difference between Hinduism and Buddhism is the Hindu belief in:

a. eternal salvation.

b. the caste system.

c. reincarnation.

d. the Buddha.

88. The varied and numerous foreign languages spoken in the United States are an example of:

a. cultural regions.

b. cultural diffusion.

c. innovation.

d. ethnicity.

89. Generally speaking, cities have expensive land, tall buildings, and crowded roads due to:

a. the birthrate.

b. low population density.

c. available land.

d. high population density.

Question 90 pertains to the following Native American oral story:

"This is the way it happened: Coyote was traveling over the plains beyond the big mountains. He came to a flat. There he found an old Buffalo skull. It was the skull of Buffalo Bull. Coyote had always been afraid of Buffalo Bull. He remembered the many times Bull Buffalo had scared him, and he laughed upon seeing the old skull there on the flat."

90. This passage is an example of:

a. ethnic groups.

b. cultural diffusion.

c. socialization.

d. assimilation.

91. The fact that Algerians and Palestinians can share the same language and religion is an example of:

a. ethnicity.

b. cultural regions.

c. cultural diversity.

d. innovation.

92. The main focus of Egyptian religion was:

    a. Puritan faith.

    b. the afterlife.

    c. heaven.

    d. reincarnation.

93. The basic tenet of Islam is that God chose:

    a. Joseph Smith as the prophet.

    b. saints to instruct others.

    c. Jesus to lead disciples.

    d. Muhammad to be his messenger to the world.

94. Some groups believe that Hebrews were the first group to practice:

    a. law.

    b. monotheism.

    c. ritual sacrifice.

    d. religion.

95. Woodrow Wilson was reelected president in 1916. A major reason for his reelection was his belief in:

    a. expansion.

    b. alliances.

    c. joining World War I.

    d. neutrality.

96. Mexico wanted to go to war with the United States in 1917 because:

    a. they wanted to join the Allies.

    b. they wanted to join Germany in the fight.

    c. they wanted to get back lands they had lost to the U.S. in 1847.

    d. they wanted to involve other countries besides those in Europe.

97. In the late 1930s, World War II began brewing when Japan invaded China and Italy invaded:

    a. Madagascar.

    b. Ethiopia.

    c. South Africa.

    d. Kenya.

98. In order to attempt to combat their poor economic standing after World War II, Germany did which of the following:

    a. It printed more money.

    b. It made an economic alliance with the U.S.

    c. It borrowed money from its former allies.

    d. It supported dictators.

99. Which was the first state in the United States that allowed 18-year-olds to vote?

    a. Missouri

    b. Connecticut

    c. Georgia

    d. California

100. The Lend-Lease Act allowed which of the following to happen?

    a. It allowed Germany to borrow money.

    b. It allowed England to borrow or lease U.S. supplies to fight against Germany.

    c. It allowed France to borrow supplies.

    d. It allowed the United States to borrow from other countries.

Answer Key and Explanations

1. C: According to TExES Competency 001, the beginning teacher "knows characteristics and uses of formal and informal oral language assessments and uses multiple, ongoing assessments to monitor and evaluate students' oral language skills." The best answer is C because it is the example of formal reading assessment as outlined in the competency.

2. B: TExES Competency 001 states that teachers "build on current oral skills to increase students' oral language proficiency." B is the answer because it correctly describes the beliefs of word recognition instruction, which are that words need to be taught in both isolation and context. The answers of either isolation or context alone do not provide the basis for increased oral language proficiency.

3. A: The teacher in this example is also following TExES Competency 001 and is teaching students to evaluate the effectiveness of their own spoken messages and the messages of others. This will increase students' reading proficiency, as the other answers cannot be achieved by the example given in this question. Therefore, the correct answer is A.

4. D: The teacher in this example models listening skills for various purposes, a crucial piece to teaching reading as stated in TExES Competency 001. The correct answer is D because in addition to modeling listening skills, the activity in this question builds on home backgrounds and cultures.

5. A: Reading aloud, or listening to a student read aloud, builds decontextualized language skills more than any of the other choices. While often increased through reading aloud, vocabulary acquisition is most often increased through constantly

reading a variety of genres. Listening skills are not necessarily strengthened through reading aloud, and the only way to improve writing skills is to write frequently in a number of different styles (e.g., poetry, prose, etc.).

6. B: This question is in line with TExES Competency 002, which says that "the teacher understands the foundations of early literacy development." The correct answer is B because the student is unable to recall prior knowledge. He is most likely able to set a purpose for his reading and read in general, but obviously without retaining any of the material.

7. C: If a student is struggling as Alan is in this example, forcing him to read more or immediate placement in the lowest reading level will not help him become a better reader. If the interventions at home and in the classroom have not worked to this point, then the child is ready for referral to a specialist. This ties in with TExES Competency 002: "the teacher knows how to use ongoing assessment to determine when a student needs additional help or intervention…"

8. C: Mnemonic devices will be the most useful in this case based on the student population. According to TExES Competency 002, a teacher understands that literacy development comes from a variety of sources. So while memorization or songs may work for some students, mnemonic devices will reach the greatest number of students.

9. D: If the student cannot read for himself, and is relying on pictures and classmates' participation, then he is in Stage 0 of reading development. (TExES Competency 002 – The teacher understands the foundations of early literacy development.) The higher stages of reading development will allow students to read for themselves, as well as read for information and retention.

10. A: Once a student reaches Stage 3 of reading, he or she will be able to read for knowledge and learning and no longer just comprehension. (TExES Competency 002) Just because a student has entered Stage 3 of reading does not mean that he or she will be able to read chapter books, study a foreign language, or become a peer tutor. While certainly the student may be able to do those things, Stage 3 is not an indicator of anything besides reading for knowledge and learning.

11. B: Students who cannot decode cannot recognize or assume meanings of unknown words. They can most likely understand some formal and newspaper writing. As stated in TExES Competency 003, the teacher "understands the importance of word identification skills (including decoding, blending, structural analysis, and sight word vocabulary) and reading fluency and provides many opportunities for students to practice and improve word identification skills and reading fluency." Therefore, the correct answer is B

12. C: While the options are beneficial, repeated reading of words in context or short phrases will best improve the high-frequency word recognition. (TExES Competency 003) Although word walls may be quite useful in the reading classroom, their presence does not guarantee high-frequency word recognition. Flash cards are undoubtedly helpful, but without context clues, they lack the benefits of reading words in short phrases. The same can be said for word banks, which are often used as a crutch by students.

13. B: TExES Competency 003 also states that the teacher "understands the connection of word identification skills and reading fluency to reading comprehension." Because of this, the correct answer is B. Also, the other answers do not give levels that are appropriate for either help or assessment.

14. A: A 90-95% accuracy in word recognition will best help the teacher with her paired reading activity. (TExES Competency 003) The other percentages will

contain texts that are above the reading level of the students in question. Good reading pedagogy tells us that a student must have a 90-95% accuracy rate in recognizing words in order to successfully participate in a paired activity.

15. B: Prefixes, suffixes, and roots are the only examples given of structural cues. (TExES Competency 003) The alphabetic principle is that letters are used to make speech sounds, while syntax is the grammatical arrangement of words in a sentence. Semantics is the study of language meaning; therefore, choices A, C, and D are not examples of structural cues.

16. D: TExES Competency 004 suggests that "the teacher understands the importance of reading for understanding, knows components and processes of reading comprehension, and teaches students strategies for improving their comprehension." Answer D is the best way for Mr. Fox to teach students strategies for improving their comprehension, as he will engage them fully in the lesson and tasks.

17. A: Current events texts will help Ms. Stone teach life skills, such as reading, in a way that will grab the students' attention. The other examples may work for some students, but choice A will certainly reach the greatest number of students. (TExES Competency 004)

18. B: The best and most effective way to assess conventions of writing (or for most rubrics) is to assess students on separate criteria over a long period of time. Then, the students can be assessed on everything as a final or culminating assignment. Assessing students only on one aspect will not follow best teaching practices or the guidelines laid out by TExES Competency 006.

19. D: Only a variety of topics and genres will allow students to best develop their proficiency. D is the correct answer because students will not become bored with a variety of topics and the other answers are too specific. (TExES Competency 006)

20. C: According to TExES Competency 007, "the teacher understands that writing to communicate is a developmental process and provides instruction that promotes students' competence in written communication." C is the correct answer because the teacher is able to help students understand how to write for a variety of audiences in a variety of settings. While the other answers are somewhat applicable here, C best answers the question.

21. C: TExES Competency 008 states that "the teacher understands skills for interpreting, analyzing, evaluating, and producing visual images and messages in various media and provides students with opportunities to develop skills in this area." Answer choice C best fits with TExES Competency 008 and is therefore the correct answer. The other answers choices are not entirely wrong, but do not offer the same range in order to help students develop the desired skills.

22. B: B is the best answer here because it most freely allows for analysis. The other choices are solid examples, but B allows students to add a personal touch to the assignment. (TExES Competency 008)

23. A: TExES Competency 009 describes the beginning teacher as one who "understands the importance of study and inquiry skills as tools for learning in the content areas and promotes students' development in applying study and inquiry skills." A is the correct answer because it allows for real life concepts and examples to come to life in the classroom, thus promoting students' development in inquiry skills.

24. A: Correctly copying from an encyclopedia or reference book or summarizing information on a graphic organizer does not help address research questions. A is the correct answer because correctly copying teacher-generated material is not an authentic learning experience, nor does it address research questions. (TExES Competency 009)

25. D: Obviously this assignment is not tedious, boring, or difficult. Therefore, the correct answer is D, meaningful instruction. (TExES Competency 009)

26. A: A student cannot be expected to read for meaning if he or she does not have rapid word recognition. Therefore, the correct answer is A. Both round robin and paired reading are activities used to bolster reading skills, so students are able to participate in those activities regardless of reading level or ability.

27. A: The reading partner clearly used context clues to help out the student. There is no mention of a dictionary, thesaurus, or teacher help in this scenario. This answer is based on TExES Competencies 001-009, with emphasis on Competency 002.

28. C: By allowing students to share real-life examples, the teacher is drawing connections between the students' prior knowledge and future learning. (TExES Competencies 001-009) While perhaps they are discussing their opinions and sharing prior knowledge, this is not the best answer to the question. Bookwork will certainly not allow students to draw many connections, and a group assignment will not foster an environment in which the whole class shares with each other.

29. C: Based on context clues, it is quite evident that Harper lacks self-esteem, as she does not believe herself to be attractive, nor does she demonstrate any of the other qualities (such as meekness, etc.). A student in stage 2 or 3 of reading development would certainly be able to draw this conclusion, as the passage

specifically states that she does not think she looks as good when she applies her own makeup. (TExES Competencies 001-009)

30. C: Reader's theater is a very effective way to communicate meaning. So while it may help the students with acting skills, that is not the teacher's goal. It will also not help to determine the strongest reader in the class. (TExES Competencies 001-009)

31. A: Oral Support Reading (OSR) most effectively allows for recognition of words and phrases. OSR involves two readers of differing levels. Over the course of reading different selections, one student will slowly withdraw support until the student can read the text independently. The other answers are not appropriate for this question, especially because literacy circles are a complementary activity to OSR. (TExES Competencies 001-009)

32. C: The tenets of Fast Start state that parents should be involved for 15 minutes nightly with their children's reading.

33. D: While poems obviously include a wide range of word choice, topics, and skills, the genre is best known for its use of literary devices. This is also what will help students improve their reading skills (Competency 003)

34. B: Oral reading certainly builds confidence, and when properly executed, it allows for a warm and engaging environment in which students are entertained by an oral reading. It does not improve intelligence, nor does it promote bad behavior. It also does not support meekness, as it helps students overcome shyness.

35. D: It is crucial for students to know how to mark and cull information from a variety of sources. While our current student population will be required to know how to use standard sources such as dictionaries, they will most likely be using the Internet for much of their research. Therefore, the correct answer is D.

36. D: Good word-learning behaviors do not include forcing students to read unknown passages without assistance. Therefore, A is not the correct answer. Providing dictionaries or answers will also not promote word-learning behaviors. Thus, the correct answer is D, as semantic maps and previewing will certainly help the students learn words.

37. B: The answer is B because acrostic poems are poems in which the first letter of the line forms words related to the theme or message, and Venn diagrams are diagrams that use circles to represent logical steps. Neither are examples of webs, group work, or teacher-led instruction.

38. A: Answer choice A is the one that fits best with TExES Competencies 001-009 and also with helping students understand unknown words. Telling students answers or asking them to look up words in dictionaries will not help them build reading skills or comprehension. Helping them to understand and use context clues will help them become life-long readers and learners.

39. D: Readers in stage 3 are able to use context clues to decipher meaning without teacher assistance. They also read for meaning and knowledge. Thus, the correct answer is D.

40. C: To summarize TExES Competencies 001-009, students learn best when given concrete, everyday examples to compare with their current reading selection. By comparing the author's word choice to the setting and purpose of the text, the teacher is allowing the students to see how language develops and is used in different groups. Therefore, C is the correct answer.

41. B: The student has obviously given an incorrect answer, but that is no reason for the teacher to call a timeout during the lesson. And while she may want to call the parents, that is not necessarily the correct answer here. Removing him from class will also not achieve anything productive. Thus, his answer should be evidence of a referral to a specialist, for at his age, he should be able to answer the teacher's simple question.

42. C: The teacher is using students' prior knowledge to draw connections between real life and what they are reading in class. Furthermore, she is allowing the students to relate to each of the characters in the passage, a task outlined in detail in TExES Competencies 001-009.

43. A: The passage is directed at a specific audience, hence the author's word choice and scenery. Not all people are interested in the same topics or genres; it would be unrealistic for the author to change syntax. It can be argued that the author is creating a setting, but A is still the most correct answer, given the passage.

44. B: The readers of this text would use context clues to surmise that "vacillate" means indecisive (if they didn't already know). "Flat", "special", or "choice", do not make sense when re-inserted into the passage in place of "vacillate". The teacher would also hopefully by this point given explicit instructions on how to use context clues to determine a word's meaning.

45. C: Moving to stage 4 will allow the student to really understand relationships among all characters. While it certainly relies on his decoding skills, as well as allows him to help his classmates, the defining characteristic of stage 4 is listed in answer choice C.

46. B: While almost all of the answer choices are applicable, the best answer is B because it allows students to call upon prior knowledge, an important aspect of reading. It is also outlined in TExES Competencies 001-009.

47. B: The author's word choice obviously informs the reader's opinion and perspective. This question is crucial in demonstrating the importance of correct word choice in writing. Character formation and relationships are undoubtedly important when reading any text, but word choice is the *best* answer to the question.

48. C: Using words in a variety of contexts is the opposite of using them in a vacuum. Students should understand that what they learn in one novel will certainly come in handy and be used again in future reading, especially if they are in the upper stages of reading development. Stereotypical context makes for boring reading and almost no improvement in reading skills. Thus, the correct answer is C.

49. A: One important aspect of reading comprehension is that, at a certain point, students will begin to understand how language gives meaning and the importance of word choice. Higher-level synonyms and words in a foreign language certainly will not help students become better readers. Also, memorizing words for a test or quiz and then promptly forgetting them absolutely does not help readers strengthen their skills.

50. D: The only way that life-long readers and learners will be created in a school is by allowing students to recognize words and concepts from the classroom in the outside world. Reading the dictionary will certainly not bring this about. Reading nightly will certainly help, but will not necessarily promote the idea that what we are learning in school has a purpose in the outside world. Thus, the answer is D.

51. A: TExES Competency 010 states that "the teacher understands and applies knowledge of significant historical events and developments, multiple historical interpretations and ideas, and relationships between the past, the present, and the future, as defined by the TEKS." The United States paid $15 for the Louisiana Purchase.

52. C: Manifest Destiny is the belief that the United States should extend from the Atlantic to the Pacific Ocean. This belief caused the forceful movement of many Indians during that time period. (TExES Competency 010)

53. D: The United States gained the land that is now California in the Mexican War. (TExES Competency 010) The Civil War, Louisiana Purchase, and War of 1812 did not involve land disputes with Mexico concerning what is now California.

54. B: Congress created both Kansas and Nebraska in 1854. (TExES Competency 010) Georgia was the 4th state in 1788; North Dakota became the 39th state in 1889; and Missouri became the 24th state in 1821.

55. C: The abolitionists and slave owners were the two main groups to rush to Kansas, because whichever side had the most support and population in the new state would be allowed to claim Kansas as a free state or a slave state. The Whigs were the opposition to the Tories, urged social reform, and promoted the American Revolution. Whigs is not the correct answer because the party did not exist in the correct time period. Suffragists advocated voting rights for women, again, a group not within the correct time period. (TExES Competency 010)

56. A: Mr. Scott was denied his right to freedom in the 1857 court case. (TExES Competency 010) He first went to trial in 1847 to sue for his freedom. He lived in the free states of Illinois and Wisconsin before moving back to the slave state of Missouri; his case went all the way to the U.S. Supreme Court.

57. D: Border states are defined as slaveholding states that bordered the free states and did not secede during the Civil War. (TExES Competency 010)

58. A: During Reconstruction, landowners were forced to pay taxes and did not have enough people to work the land. Furthermore, they did not have enough money to pay the workers they did have. (TExES Competency 010)

59. C: Carpetbaggers were non-southerners who came to the South during the Reconstruction Era between 1865 and 1877 to take advantage of and profit from the defeated southerners. They carried bags made of carpet material, and were very commonly referred to as vultures. (TExES Competency 010)

60. B: TExES Competency 011 states that "the teacher understands and applies knowledge of geographic relationships involving people, places, and environments in Texas, the United States, and the world, as defined by the TEKS." Absolute location is defined as the exact spot on the earth's surface where a place is found.

61. D: Landforms, such as mountains, directly affect the living and working habits of the inhabitants of an area. (TExES Competency 011) Erosion is the mechanical process of wearing or grinding something down; weathering is the decomposition of earth and soil through contact with the planet's forces; and location is defined as the point occupied on the earth's surface. Thus, landforms is the correct answer as it is the only one that affects living and working habits.

62. B: Two continental plates crashing together form mountains. (TExES Competency 011) Magma is molten rock in the earth's crust, and so would not form mountains within the earth's crust.

63. A: While the other answers are certainly important, we need to focus (especially now in this economy) on how the economies of major financial centers affect the rest of the world. Thus, A is the correct answer. (TExES Competency 011)

64. A: Volcanoes, water, sun, and snow certainly are causes of landform erosion; however, wind and glaciers are the two leading causes, and westerlies and trade winds have more to do with sailing and shipping than erosion. (TExES Competency 011)

65. C: Prevailing winds are winds that blow in the same direction over large areas of earth. (TExES Competency 011)

66. D: Tundras are coasts in high latitudes. (TExES Competency 011)

67. C: TExES Competency 12 states that the teacher "understands and applies knowledge of economic systems and how people organize economic systems to produce, distribute, and consume goods and services, as defined by the TEKS." A command economy is defined as an economy that is completely controlled by the government.

68. C: The railroads became an integral part of the economic and population expansion in the early 1800s in the United States. (TExES Competency 012) Reconstruction occurred during a time period that would preclude if from being the correct answer.

69. B: The first national railroad occurred in England. (TExES Competency 012)

70. B: China's economy is completely controlled by its government. Thus, choice B is the correct answer. (TExES Competency 012) India's government is known as the Union Government and was established by the Constitution of India. Egypt has

been a republic since 1953, and has a president as well as a People's Assembly and National Democratic Party. The United States is of course a democracy.

71. A: The four basic principles of the free enterprise system are profit motive of owners, private property rights, freedom of choice, and owner control. (TExES Competency 012)

72. C: Unemployment changes the value of the dollar as well as the amount that each person in the economy earns and, therefore, has to spend. In short, it affects the amount of goods and services that consumers are willing and able to buy. In a bad economy, people are not willing to spend money on disposable goods or expendable items. (TExES Competency 12)

73. C: A mixed economy is a combination of traditional, command, and market economies. (TExES Competency 012)

74. B: Interdependence is defined as being dependent on one another for certain needs. The automobile industry is an example of interdependence because automobiles are made in several states and even several countries, with each location providing a different good or service. (TExES Competency 012)

75. D: While the assembly line certainly revolutionized and sped up production, it also led to a loss of independence, as workers could see only the specific item they were making at that point in the line and often did not see the finished product. (TExES Competency 012)

76. C: TExES Competency 013 defines the beginning teacher as able to "understand and apply knowledge of government, democracy and citizenship, including ways in which the individuals and groups achieve their goals through political systems, as defined by TEKS." The presidential veto power is an example of checks and

balances, which was put into place so no one branch of the government would become more powerful than another.

77. D: This quote is found in the Bill of Rights, which is the first Ten Amendments to the Constitution. (TExES Competency 013) That statement is not seen in the Texas Constitution, nor in the Articles of Confederation, which was the first draft of the Constitution agreed upon by the first thirteen states. The Constitution embodies our governing principles. Therefore, the correct answer is D.

78. C: Two-thirds of each House must propose and ¾ of the states must ratify an Amendment to the Constitution. (TExES Competency 013)

79. A: Federalism is defined as the political system in which the national government is supreme but shares some powers with state governments, which also have certain independent powers. This became the operating system of the United States after the Civil War. (TExES Competency 013)

80. B: Many railroads and corporations became too dominant and monopolizing in the United States in the early 1900s, thus leading to the passage of the Sherman Anti-Trust Act. (TExES Competency 013)

81. A: The court ruled in Brown v. Board of Education (1954) that all children were entitled to the same public education, regardless of race or ethnicity. (TExES Competency 013)

82. C: In both the Sherman Anti-Trust Act and Brown v. Board of Education, the federal government increased its power. (TExES Competency 013)

83. C: The money given to states during the New Deal certainly came with strings attached; the states had to accept federal regulations if they wanted to use the federal government's money. (TExES Competency 013)

84. D: Each Amendment in the Bill of Rights was written to increase the democracy already contained in the Constitution. (TExES Competency 013)

85. B: Marbury v. Madison established judicial review, an extremely important decision because it allowed more opportunities to support the checks and balances system upheld by the federal government. (TExES Competency 013)

86. B: TExES Competency 14 states that the beginning teacher "understands and applies knowledge of cultural development, adaptation, and diversity, and understands and applies knowledge of interactions among science, technology, and society, as defined by TEKS." The biggest difference between the U.S. and India is the presence of the caste system in India, which Americans do not subscribe to.

87. C: A cornerstone of Hinduism is reincarnation, while Buddhists believe in the Buddha. Although there are numerous similarities and differences between the two religions, more detail is not necessary for this particular question. (TExES Competency 014)

88. B: Cultural diffusion is the act of spreading and accepting different cultures in more than one cultural region or geographic area. Thus, the correct answer is B. (TExES Competency 014)

89. D: High population density leads to a high demand in real estate, thus driving the market prices higher. Therefore, the answer is D. (TExES Competency 014)

90. B: Please see the answer to number 88.

91. C: Cultural diversity is defined as more than one ethnic group sharing the same basic beliefs or cultural practices. This explains the fact that Algerians and Palestinians can both practice the same religion. (TExES Competency 014)

92. B: Egyptians believed wholeheartedly in the afterlife, and based all of their life and burial rituals on this belief. (TExES Competency 014)

93. D: Islamic followers believe that Muhammad was chosen by God to be his messenger on earth. Thus, D is the correct answer. Joseph Smith is the leader of Mormons and Jesus the leader of Christians. (TExES Competency 014)

94. B: Hebrews were the first group to practice monotheism, or the belief in only one God. (TExES Competency 014)

95. D: TExES Competency 015 states that the beginning teacher "understands the foundations of social studies education and applies knowledge of skills used in the social sciences." During this time in United States history, most American followed a policy of neutrality and reelected President Wilson because he believed the same.

96. C: Mexico's main reason for wanting to join the war was to earn back lands they had lost almost a century earlier. (TExES Competency 015)

97. C: Italy invaded Ethiopia, an invasion that certainly contributed to the quick spread of World War II. (TExES Competency 015)

98. A: Germany printed more money in an ill-advised attempt to rescue their floundering economy. This action contributed to further downfall of the once powerful nation, and also contributed to the rise of Hitler during World War II. (TExES Competency 015)

99. B: Connecticut was the first state to allow 18-year-olds to vote, ostensibly because they were also deemed old enough to be drafted for war. (TExES Competency 015) All states ratified the amendment in 1971, but Connecticut was the first state to do so.

100. B: Despite Wilson's neutrality policy in the earlier war, the United States allowed England to lease supplies in order to fight against Germany. (TExES Competency 015)

Special Report: What Your Test Score Will Tell You About Your IQ

Did you know that most standardized tests correlate very strongly with IQ? In fact, your general intelligence is a better predictor of your success than any other factor, and most tests intentionally measure this trait to some degree to ensure that those selected by the test are truly qualified for the test's purposes.

Before we can delve into the relation between your test score and IQ, I will first have to explain what exactly is IQ. Here's the formula:

Your IQ = 100 + (Number of standard deviations below or above the average)*15

Now, let's define standard deviations by using an example. If we have 5 people with 5 different heights, then first we calculate the average. Let's say the average was 65 inches. The standard deviation is the "average distance" away from the average of each of the members. It is a direct measure of variability - if the 5 people included Jackie Chan and Shaquille O'Neal, obviously there's a lot more variability in that group than a group of 5 sisters who are all within 6 inches in height of each other. The standard deviation uses a number to characterize the average range of difference within a group.

A convenient feature of most groups is that they have a "normal" distribution- makes sense that most things would be normal, right? Without getting into a bunch of statistical mumbo-jumbo, you just need to know that if you know the average of the group and the standard deviation, you can successfully predict someone's percentile rank in the group.

Confused? Let me give you an example. If instead of 5 people's heights, we had 100 people, we could figure out their rank in height JUST by knowing the average, standard deviation, and their height. We wouldn't need to know each person's height and manually rank them, we could just predict their rank based on three numbers.

What this means is that you can take your PERCENTILE rank that is often given with your test and relate this to your RELATIVE IQ of people taking the test - that is, your IQ relative to the people taking the test. Obviously, there's no way to know your actual IQ because the people taking a standardized test are usually not very good samples of the general population- many of those with extremely low IQ's never achieve a level of success or competency necessary to complete a typical standardized test. In fact, professional psychologists who measure IQ actually have to use non-written tests that can fairly measure the IQ of those not able to complete a traditional test.

The bottom line is to not take your test score too seriously, but it is fun to compute your "relative IQ" among the people who took the test with you. I've done the calculations below. Just look up your percentile rank in the left and then you'll see your "relative IQ" for your test in the right hand column-

Percentile Rank	Your Relative IQ		Percentile Rank	Your Relative IQ
99	135		59	103
98	131		58	103
97	128		57	103
96	126		56	102
95	125		55	102
94	123		54	102
93	122		53	101
92	121		52	101
91	120		51	100
90	119		50	100
89	118		49	100
88	118		48	99
87	117		47	99
86	116		46	98
85	116		45	98
84	115		44	98
83	114		43	97
82	114		42	97
81	113		41	97
80	113		40	96
79	112		39	96
78	112		38	95
77	111		37	95
76	111		36	95
75	110		35	94
74	110		34	94
73	109		33	93
72	109		32	93
71	108		31	93
70	108		30	92
69	107		29	92
68	107		28	91
67	107		27	91
66	106		26	90
65	106		25	90
64	105		24	89
63	105		23	89
62	105		22	88
61	104		21	88
60	104		20	87

Special Report: Retaking the Test: What Are Your Chances at Improving Your Score?

After going through the experience of taking a major test, many test takers feel that once is enough. The test usually comes during a period of transition in the test taker's life, and taking the test is only one of a series of important events. With so many distractions and conflicting recommendations, it may be difficult for a test taker to rationally determine whether or not he should retake the test after viewing his scores.

The importance of the test usually only adds to the burden of the retake decision. However, don't be swayed by emotion. There a few simple questions that you can ask yourself to guide you as you try to determine whether a retake would improve your score:

1. What went wrong? Why wasn't your score what you expected?

Can you point to a single factor or problem that you feel caused the low score? Were you sick on test day? Was there an emotional upheaval in your life that caused a distraction? Were you late for the test or not able to use the full time allotment? If you can point to any of these specific, individual problems, then a retake should definitely be considered.

2. Is there enough time to improve?

Many problems that may show up in your score report may take a lot of time for improvement. A deficiency in a particular math skill may require weeks or months of tutoring and studying to improve. If you have enough time to improve an identified weakness, then a retake should definitely be considered.

3. How will additional scores be used? Will a score average, highest score, or most recent score be used?

Different test scores may be handled completely differently. If you've taken the test multiple times, sometimes your highest score is used, sometimes your average score is computed and used, and sometimes your most recent score is used. Make sure you understand what method will be used to evaluate your scores, and use that to help you determine whether a retake should be considered.

4. Are my practice test scores significantly higher than my actual test score?

If you have taken a lot of practice tests and are consistently scoring at a much higher level than your actual test score, then you should consider a retake. However, if you've taken five practice tests and only one of your scores was higher than your actual test score, or if your practice test scores were only slightly higher than your actual test score, then it is unlikely that you will significantly increase your score.

5. Do I need perfect scores or will I be able to live with this score? Will this score still allow me to follow my dreams?

What kind of score is acceptable to you? Is your current score "good enough?" Do you have to have a certain score in order to pursue the future of your dreams? If you won't be happy with your current score, and there's no way that you could live with it, then you should consider a retake. However, don't get your hopes up. If you are looking for significant improvement, that may or may not be possible. But if you won't be happy otherwise, it is at least worth the effort.

Remember that there are other considerations. To achieve your dream, it is likely that your grades may also be taken into account. A great test score is usually not the only thing necessary to succeed. Make sure that you aren't overemphasizing the importance of a high test score.

Furthermore, a retake does not always result in a higher score. Some test takers will score lower on a retake, rather than higher. One study shows that one-fourth of test takers will achieve a significant improvement in test score, while one-sixth of test takers will actually show a decrease. While this shows that most test takers will improve, the majority will only improve their scores a little and a retake may not be worth the test taker's effort.

Finally, if a test is taken only once and is considered in the added context of good grades on the part of a test taker, the person reviewing the grades and scores may be tempted to assume that the test taker just had a bad day while taking the test, and may discount the low test score in favor of the high grades. But if the test is retaken and the scores are approximately the same, then the validity of the low scores are only confirmed. Therefore, a retake could actually hurt a test taker by definitely bracketing a test taker's score ability to a limited range.

Special Report: What is Test Anxiety and How to Overcome It?

The very nature of tests caters to some level of anxiety, nervousness or tension, just as we feel for any important event that occurs in our lives. A little bit of anxiety or nervousness can be a good thing. It helps us with motivation, and makes achievement just that much sweeter. However, too much anxiety can be a problem; especially if it hinders our ability to function and perform.

"Test anxiety," is the term that refers to the emotional reactions that some test-takers experience when faced with a test or exam. Having a fear of testing and exams is based upon a rational fear, since the test-taker's performance can shape the course of an academic career. Nevertheless, experiencing excessive fear of examinations will only interfere with the test-takers ability to perform, and his/her chances to be successful.

There are a large variety of causes that can contribute to the development and sensation of test anxiety. These include, but are not limited to lack of performance and worrying about issues surrounding the test.

Lack of Preparation

Lack of preparation can be identified by the following behaviors or situations:

Not scheduling enough time to study, and therefore cramming the night before the test or exam

Managing time poorly, to create the sensation that there is not enough time to do everything

Failing to organize the text information in advance, so that the study material consists of the entire text and not simply the pertinent information

Poor overall studying habits

Worrying, on the other hand, can be related to both the test taker, or many other factors around him/her that will be affected by the results of the test. These include worrying about:

Previous performances on similar exams, or exams in general

How friends and other students are achieving

The negative consequences that will result from a poor grade or failure

There are three primary elements to test anxiety. Physical components, which involve the same typical bodily reactions as those to acute anxiety (to be discussed below). Emotional factors have to do with fear or panic. Mental or cognitive issues concerning attention spans and memory abilities.

Physical Signals

There are many different symptoms of test anxiety, and these are not limited to mental and emotional strain. Frequently there are a range of physical signals that will let a test taker know that he/she is suffering from test anxiety. These bodily changes can include the following:

Perspiring

Sweaty palms

Wet, trembling hands

Nausea

Dry mouth

A knot in the stomach

Headache

Faintness

Muscle tension

Aching shoulders, back and neck

Rapid heart beat

Feeling too hot/cold

To recognize the sensation of test anxiety, a test-taker should monitor him/herself for the following sensations:

The physical distress symptoms as listed above

Emotional sensitivity, expressing emotional feelings such as the need to cry or laugh too much, or a sensation of anger or helplessness

A decreased ability to think, causing the test-taker to blank out or have racing thoughts that are hard to organize or control.

Though most students will feel some level of anxiety when faced with a test or exam, the majority can cope with that anxiety and maintain it at a manageable level. However, those who cannot are faced with a very real and very serious condition, which can and should be controlled for the immeasurable benefit of this sufferer.

Naturally, these sensations lead to negative results for the testing experience. The most common effects of test anxiety have to do with nervousness and mental blocking.

Nervousness

Nervousness can appear in several different levels:

The test-taker's difficulty, or even inability to read and understand the questions on the test

The difficulty or inability to organize thoughts to a coherent form

The difficulty or inability to recall key words and concepts relating to the testing questions (especially essays)

The receipt of poor grades on a test, though the test material was well known by the test taker

Conversely, a person may also experience mental blocking, which involves:

Blanking out on test questions

Only remembering the correct answers to the questions when the test has already finished.

Fortunately for test anxiety sufferers, beating these feelings, to a large degree, has to do with proper preparation. When a test taker has a feeling of preparedness, then anxiety will be dramatically lessened.

The first step to resolving anxiety issues is to distinguish which of the two types of anxiety are being suffered. If the anxiety is a direct result of a lack of preparation, this should be considered a normal reaction, and the anxiety level (as opposed to the test results) shouldn't be anything to worry about. However, if, when adequately prepared, the test-taker still panics, blanks out, or seems to overreact, this is not a fully rational reaction. While this can be considered normal too, there are many ways to combat and overcome these effects.

Remember that anxiety cannot be entirely eliminated, however, there are ways to minimize it, to make the anxiety easier to manage. Preparation is one of the best ways to minimize test anxiety. Therefore the following techniques are wise in order to best fight off any anxiety that may want to build.

To begin with, try to avoid cramming before a test, whenever it is possible. By trying to memorize an entire term's worth of information in one day, you'll be shocking your system, and not giving yourself a very good chance to absorb the information. This is an easy path to anxiety, so for those who suffer from test anxiety, cramming should not even be considered an option.

Instead of cramming, work throughout the semester to combine all of the material which is presented throughout the semester, and work on it gradually as the course goes by, making sure to master the main concepts first, leaving minor details for a week or so before the test.

To study for the upcoming exam, be sure to pose questions that may be on the examination, to gauge the ability to answer them by integrating the ideas from your texts, notes and lectures, as well as any supplementary readings.

If it is truly impossible to cover all of the information that was covered in that particular term, concentrate on the most important portions, that can be covered very well. Learn these concepts as best as possible, so that when the test comes, a goal can be made to use these concepts as presentations of your knowledge.

In addition to study habits, changes in attitude are critical to beating a struggle with test anxiety. In fact, an improvement of the perspective over the entire test-taking experience can actually help a test taker to enjoy studying and therefore improve the overall experience. Be certain not to overemphasize the significance of the grade - know that the result of the test is neither a reflection of self worth, nor is it a measure of intelligence; one grade will not predict a person's future success.

To improve an overall testing outlook, the following steps should be tried:

Keeping in mind that the most reasonable expectation for taking a test is to expect to try to demonstrate as much of what you know as you possibly can. Reminding ourselves that a test is only one test; this is not the only one, and there will be others.
The thought of thinking of oneself in an irrational, all-or-nothing term should be avoided at all costs.
A reward should be designated for after the test, so there's something to look forward to. Whether it be going to a movie, going out to eat, or simply visiting friends, schedule it in advance, and do it no matter what result is expected on the exam.

Test-takers should also keep in mind that the basics are some of the most important things, even beyond anti-anxiety techniques and studying. Never neglect the basic social, emotional and biological needs, in order to try to absorb information. In order to best achieve, these three factors must be held as just as important as the studying itself.

Study Steps

Remember the following important steps for studying:

Maintain healthy nutrition and exercise habits. Continue both your recreational activities and social pass times. These both contribute to your physical and emotional well being.

Be certain to get a good amount of sleep, especially the night before the test, because when you're overtired you are not able to perform to the best of your best ability.

Keep the studying pace to a moderate level by taking breaks when they are needed, and varying the work whenever possible, to keep the mind fresh instead of getting bored.

When enough studying has been done that all the material that can be learned has been learned, and the test taker is prepared for the test, stop studying and do something relaxing such as listening to music, watching a movie, or taking a warm bubble bath.

There are also many other techniques to minimize the uneasiness or apprehension that is experienced along with test anxiety before, during, or even after the examination. In fact, there are a great deal of things that can be done to stop anxiety from interfering with lifestyle and performance. Again, remember that anxiety will not be eliminated entirely, and it shouldn't be. Otherwise that "up" feeling for exams would not exist, and most of us depend on that sensation to perform better than usual. However, this anxiety has to be at a level that is manageable.

Of course, as we have just discussed, being prepared for the exam is half the battle right away. Attending all classes, finding out what knowledge will be expected on the exam, and knowing the exam schedules are easy steps to lowering anxiety. Keeping up with work will remove the need to cram, and efficient study habits will eliminate wasted time. Studying should be done in an ideal location for concentration, so that it is simple to become interested in the

- 134 -

material and give it complete attention. A method such as SQ3R (Survey, Question, Read, Recite, Review) is a wonderful key to follow to make sure that the study habits are as effective as possible, especially in the case of learning from a textbook. Flashcards are great techniques for memorization. Learning to take good notes will mean that notes will be full of useful information, so that less sifting will need to be done to seek out what is pertinent for studying. Reviewing notes after class and then again on occasion will keep the information fresh in the mind. From notes that have been taken summary sheets and outlines can be made for simpler reviewing.

A study group can also be a very motivational and helpful place to study, as there will be a sharing of ideas, all of the minds can work together, to make sure that everyone understands, and the studying will be made more interesting because it will be a social occasion.

Basically, though, as long as the test-taker remains organized and self confident, with efficient study habits, less time will need to be spent studying, and higher grades will be achieved.

To become self confident, there are many useful steps. The first of these is "self talk." It has been shown through extensive research, that self-talk for students who suffer from test anxiety, should be well monitored, in order to make sure that it contributes to self confidence as opposed to sinking the student. Frequently the self talk of test-anxious students is negative or self-defeating, thinking that everyone else is smarter and faster, that they always mess up, and that if they don't do well, they'll fail the entire course. It is important to decreasing anxiety that awareness is made of self talk. Try writing any negative self thoughts and then disputing them with a positive statement instead. Begin self-encouragement as though it was a friend speaking. Repeat positive statements to help reprogram the mind to believing in successes instead of failures.

Helpful Techniques

Other extremely helpful techniques include:

Self-visualization of doing well and reaching goals

While aiming for an "A" level of understanding, don't try to "overprotect" by setting your expectations lower. This will only convince the mind to stop studying in order to meet the lower expectations.

Don't make comparisons with the results or habits of other students. These are individual factors, and different things work for different people, causing different results.

Strive to become an expert in learning what works well, and what can be done in order to improve. Consider collecting this data in a journal.

Create rewards for after studying instead of doing things before studying that will only turn into avoidance behaviors.

Make a practice of relaxing - by using methods such as progressive relaxation, self-hypnosis, guided imagery, etc - in order to make relaxation an automatic sensation.

Work on creating a state of relaxed concentration so that concentrating will take on the focus of the mind, so that none will be wasted on worrying.

Take good care of the physical self by eating well and getting enough sleep.

Plan in time for exercise and stick to this plan.

Beyond these techniques, there are other methods to be used before, during and after the test that will help the test-taker perform well in addition to overcoming anxiety.

Before the exam comes the academic preparation. This involves establishing a study schedule and beginning at least one week before the actual date of the test. By doing this, the anxiety of not having enough time to study for the test will be automatically eliminated. Moreover, this will make the studying a much more effective experience, ensuring that the learning will be an easier process. This relieves much undue pressure on the test-taker.

Summary sheets, note cards, and flash cards with the main concepts and examples of these main concepts should be prepared in advance of the actual studying time. A topic should never be eliminated from this process. By omitting a topic because it isn't expected to be on the test is only setting up the test-taker for anxiety should it actually appear on the exam. Utilize the course syllabus for laying out the topics that should be studied. Carefully go over the notes that were made in class, paying special attention to any of the issues that the professor took special care to emphasize while lecturing in class. In the textbooks, use the chapter review, or if possible, the chapter tests, to begin your review.

It may even be possible to ask the instructor what information will be covered on the exam, or what the format of the exam will be (for example, multiple choice, essay, free form, true-false). Additionally, see if it is possible to find out how many questions will be on the test. If a review sheet or sample test has been offered by the professor, make good use of it, above anything else, for the preparation for the test. Another great resource for getting to know the examination is reviewing tests from previous semesters. Use these tests to review, and aim to achieve a 100% score on each of the possible topics. With a few exceptions, the goal that you set for yourself is the highest one that you will reach.

Take all of the questions that were assigned as homework, and rework them to any other possible course material. The more problems reworked, the more skill and confidence will form as a result. When forming the solution to a problem, write out each of the steps. Don't simply do head work. By doing as many steps on paper as possible, much clarification and therefore confidence will be formed. Do this with as many homework problems as possible, before checking the answers. By checking the answer after each problem, a reinforcement will exist, that will not be on the exam. Study situations should be as exam-like as possible, to prime the test-taker's system for the experience. By waiting to check the answers at the end, a psychological advantage will be formed, to decrease the stress factor.

Another fantastic reason for not cramming is the avoidance of confusion in concepts, especially when it comes to mathematics. 8-10 hours of study will become one hundred percent more effective if it is spread out over a week or at least several days, instead of doing it all in one sitting. Recognize that the human brain requires time in order to assimilate new material, so frequent breaks and a span of study time over several days will be much more beneficial.

Additionally, don't study right up until the point of the exam. Studying should stop a minimum of one hour before the exam begins. This allows the brain to rest and put things in their proper order. This will also provide the time to become as relaxed as possible when going into the examination room. The test-taker will also have time to eat well and eat sensibly. Know that the brain needs food as much as the rest of the body. With enough food and enough sleep, as well as a relaxed attitude, the body and the mind are primed for success.

Avoid any anxious classmates who are talking about the exam. These students only spread anxiety, and are not worth sharing the anxious sentimentalities.

Before the test also involves creating a positive attitude, so mental preparation should also be a point of concentration. There are many keys to creating a positive attitude. Should fears become rushing in, make a visualization of taking the exam, doing well, and seeing an A written on the paper. Write out a list of affirmations that will bring a feeling of confidence, such as "I am doing well in my English class," "I studied well and know my material," "I enjoy this class." Even if the affirmations aren't believed at first, it sends a positive message to the subconscious which will result in an alteration of the overall belief system, which is the system that creates reality.

If a sensation of panic begins, work with the fear and imagine the very worst! Work through the entire scenario of not passing the test, failing the entire course, and dropping out of school, followed by not getting a job, and pushing a shopping cart through the dark alley where you'll live. This will place things into perspective! Then, practice deep breathing and create a visualization of the opposite situation - achieving an "A" on the exam, passing the entire course, receiving the degree at a graduation ceremony.

On the day of the test, there are many things to be done to ensure the best results, as well as the most calm outlook. The following stages are suggested in order to maximize test-taking potential:

Begin the examination day with a moderate breakfast, and avoid any coffee or beverages with caffeine if the test taker is prone to jitters. Even people who are used to managing caffeine can feel jittery or light-headed when it is taken on a test day.
Attempt to do something that is relaxing before the examination begins. As last minute cramming clouds the mastering of overall concepts, it is better to use this time to create a calming outlook.

Be certain to arrive at the test location well in advance, in order to provide time to select a location that is away from doors, windows and other distractions, as well as giving enough time to relax before the test begins.

Keep away from anxiety generating classmates who will upset the sensation of stability and relaxation that is being attempted before the exam.

Should the waiting period before the exam begins cause anxiety, create a self-distraction by reading a light magazine or something else that is relaxing and simple.

During the exam itself, read the entire exam from beginning to end, and find out how much time should be allotted to each individual problem. Once writing the exam, should more time be taken for a problem, it should be abandoned, in order to begin another problem. If there is time at the end, the unfinished problem can always be returned to and completed.

Read the instructions very carefully - twice - so that unpleasant surprises won't follow during or after the exam has ended.

When writing the exam, pretend that the situation is actually simply the completion of homework within a library, or at home. This will assist in forming a relaxed atmosphere, and will allow the brain extra focus for the complex thinking function.

Begin the exam with all of the questions with which the most confidence is felt. This will build the confidence level regarding the entire exam and will begin a quality momentum. This will also create encouragement for trying the problems where uncertainty resides.

Going with the "gut instinct" is always the way to go when solving a problem. Second guessing should be avoided at all costs. Have confidence in the ability to do well.

For essay questions, create an outline in advance that will keep the mind organized and make certain that all of the points are remembered. For multiple choice, read every answer, even if the correct one has been spotted - a better one may exist.

Continue at a pace that is reasonable and not rushed, in order to be able to work carefully. Provide enough time to go over the answers at the end, to check for small errors that can be corrected.

Should a feeling of panic begin, breathe deeply, and think of the feeling of the body releasing sand through its pores. Visualize a calm, peaceful place, and include all of the sights, sounds and sensations of this image. Continue the deep breathing, and take a few minutes to continue this with closed eyes. When all is well again, return to the test.

If a "blanking" occurs for a certain question, skip it and move on to the next question. There will be time to return to the other question later. Get everything done that can be done, first, to guarantee all the grades that can be compiled, and to build all of the confidence possible. Then return to the weaker questions to build the marks from there.

Remember, one's own reality can be created, so as long as the belief is there, success will follow. And remember: anxiety can happen later, right now, there's an exam to be written!

After the examination is complete, whether there is a feeling for a good grade or a bad grade, don't dwell on the exam, and be certain to follow through on the reward that was promised...and enjoy it! Don't dwell on any mistakes that have been made, as there is nothing that can be done at this point anyway.

Additionally, don't begin to study for the next test right away. Do something relaxing for a while, and let the mind relax and prepare itself to begin absorbing information again.

From the results of the exam - both the grade and the entire experience, be certain to learn from what has gone on. Perfect studying habits and work some more on confidence in order to make the next examination experience even better than the last one.

Learn to avoid places where openings occurred for laziness, procrastination and day dreaming.

Use the time between this exam and the next one to better learn to relax, even learning to relax on cue, so that any anxiety can be controlled during the next exam. Learn how to relax the body. Slouch in your chair if that helps. Tighten and then relax all of the different muscle groups, one group at a time, beginning with the feet and then working all the way up to the neck and face. This will ultimately relax the muscles more than they were to begin with. Learn how to breathe deeply and comfortably, and focus on this breathing going in and out as a relaxing thought. With every exhale, repeat the word "relax."

As common as test anxiety is, it is very possible to overcome it. Make yourself one of the test-takers who overcome this frustrating hindrance.

Special Report: Additional Bonus Material

Due to our efforts to try to keep this book to a manageable length, we've created a link that will give you access to all of your additional bonus material.

Please visit http://www.mo-media.com/texes/bonuses to access the information.